COMPUTERIZED RESERVATIONS SYSTEMS (CRSs) IN THE AIR TRANSPORT INDUSTRY

This book is due for return not later than the last
date stamped below, unless recalled sooner.

COMPUTERIZED RESERVATIONS SYSTEMS IN THE AIR TRANSPORT INDUSTRY

HOW TO OPTIMIZE THE PASSENGER'S BENEFITS

Dr. iur. utr. P. Nikolai Ehlers, LL.M.
Rechtsanwalt, Munich and Attorney at Law, New York

Kluwer Law and Taxations Publishers
Deventer · Antwerp
London · Frankfurt · Boston · New York

Distribution in the USA and Canada
Kluwer Law and Taxation Publishers
101 Philip Drive
Norwell, MA 02061
USA

Library of Congress Cataloging-in-Publication Data

Ehlers, P. Nikolai
Computerized reservations systems (CRSs): how to optimize the passenger's benefits / P. Nikolai
Ehlers.
  p.   cm.
Bibliography: p.
ISBN 9065443576
1. Aeronautics, Commercial--Law and legislation - -United States.
2. Aeronautics, Commercial--Law and legislation--Europe.
3. Airlines--United States--Reservations--Data processing.
4. Airlines--Europe--Reservations--Data processing. I. title.
K4115.4.E35 1988
343'.0977--dc19
[342.3977]   87-3537
                                                                                                CIP

D/1988/2664/26
ISBN 90 6544 357 6

© 1988 Kluwer Law and Taxation Publishers, Deventer, Netherlands

To Wawy

ABSTRACT

Since computerized reservations systems (CRSs) were first made available to travel agents in the late 1970s they have become marketing tools of unmatched importance. Airlines (as well as other vendors of services for travellers), travel agents and passengers benefit from the unsurpassed speed and comfort of CRSs with respect to information, booking, ticket printing and travel agency management support.

But the amazing capabilities of CRSs and the dependence of a whole industry on them has also vested the CRS vendors with substantial market power. The CRS vendors often have not been able to resist abusing this market power in order to gain unfair advantages over their competitors.

Currently many organizations, from the governmental as well as from the private sector, are studying the CRS situation, sometimes with a view to making recommendations for rulemaking or to promulgating such rules. This study attempts to identify the passenger's interests with respect to CRSs and to analyze policy options with a view to optimizing the passenger's benefits.

SOMMAIRE

Depuis que les systèmes de réservations par ordinateurs (SRO) ont été mis à la disposition des agences de voyages, à la fin des années 1970, ils sont devenus des outils de commercialisation d'une importance inégalée. Les compagnies aériennes (et autres vendeurs de services de voyages), les agences de voyages et les voyageurs bénéficient de la rapidité sans précédent et de la commodité des SRO pour obtenir des renseignements; faire des réservations; imprimer les billets et effectuer tout le travail de soutien des agences de voyages.

Cependant, les possibilités incomparables des SRO et le fait que toute une industrie en dépende ont permis aux vendeurs de SRO d'influencer largement le marché. Trop souvent, ils n'ont pu s'empêcher d'abuser de leur pouvoir pour s'arroger, au détriment de leurs concurrents, des privilèges injustifiables.

Présentement, plusieurs organisations, dans les secteurs tant gouvernemental que privé, étudient cette question, en vue, dans certains cas, de faire des recommandations relatives à la promulgation de règles ou à l'élaboration d'une réglementation en la matière. La présente étude tente d'identifier l'intérêt des voyageurs à utiliser les SRO, et d'analyser les différentes politiques susceptibles de maximiser les avantages qu'ils en retirent.

ACKNOWLEDGMENTS

This work would not have been possible without the deeply appreciated willingness of many to afford me their time and answer my questions. There were too many as to name everyone of them individually, but I want to express my gratitude for their ready support.

The paper is based on a thesis which was submitted in September 1987 after one year of studies at the Institute of Air and Space Law, McGill University, Montreal (Canada). I would like to thank the Director of this great institution, Dr. Nicolas Mateesco Matte, OC QC FRSC, as well as the other faculty members and fellow students for the inspiration I received there. I am particularly grateful for the help and cooperation that I experienced from Professor Peter P.C. Haanappel, the supervisor of my thesis.

The German Academic Exchange Service (DAAD) awarded me a scholarship for my LL.M. studies at the Institute of Air and Space Law, McGill University, for which I would like to thank, too.

Instrumental in this project was the scholarship and other assistance I was granted by IFAPA (Geneva).

However, without the endurance and understanding of my fiancée Elisabeth Söling, I would not have been able to spend this productive year in Canada.

I have dedicated this book to Waltraud Kalsbach-van Gerfsheim whose love and affection are a continuing essential in the lives of three men.

The information contained in this work is up-to-date until early August 1987. In a few instances, though, more recent developments could be taken into consideration.

P. Nikolai Ehlers

TABLE OF CONTENTS

LIST OF ABBREVIATIONS

AEA	Association of European Airlines
AIRINC	Aeronautical Radio Incorporated
ARC	Airline Reporting Corporation
ATA	Air Transport Association
ATB	Automated Ticket and Boarding Pass
CAB	Civil Aeronautics Board
CRS	Computerized Reservations System
CRT	Cathode Ray Tube
DOT	U.S. Department of Transportation
EC	European Communities
ECAC	European Civil Aviation Conference
EEC	European Economic Community
IATA	Inernational Air Transport Association
IBI	Intergovernmental Bureau of Informatics
ICAO	International Civil Aviation Organization
OECD	Organisation for Economic Co-Operation and Development
PNR	Passenger Name Record
SELA	Sistema Economico Latino-Americano
SITA	Société Internationale de Télécommunications Aéronautiques
TDF	Transborder Data Flow
UFTAA	Universal Federation of Travel Agents' Associations
UNCTAD	United Nations Conference on Trade and Development
UNCTC	United Nations Centre on Transnational Corporations

INTRODUCTION

CRS stands for computerized reservations system, i.e. an automated method, including equipment and programmes, for performing reservations functions and possibly for the issuance of tickets.[1] While this is a technically correct definition, in reality CRS means much more that this for the air transport industry. CRS means more than 20 years of research and development – at first in order to facilitate the airlines' reservations by substituting an automated method for the traditional manual one, and once this automated method was in operation by improving it. CRS means investments of huge dimensions: expenditures through 1990 by U.S. airlines may run as high as $4 billion for CRS hardware and software alone.[2] CRS means an opportunity for high profits: American Airlines' Sabre system produced a $142.6 million operating profit in 1985 on revenues of $335.7 million; these revenues are rental payments of travel agents for the installed equipment and booking fees of those airlines whose flights were booked through Sabre (presently $1.75 per booked flight segment) as well as payments for other services. CRS means a dense network linking airlines, travel agents, and many more in the transport and tourism industries: the U.S. vendors have more than 33.000 agency installations with approximately 130.000 CRTs.[3] CRS also means the handling of a myriad of data at the highest speed: Sabre, the system of American Airlines,[4] is capable of handling circa 1500 messages per second. The system contains schedule information for more than 650 airlines worldwide as wel as 25 million air fares. Reservations can be made through Sabre on 291 different carriers, more than 11.000 hotel and condominium properties and 21 car rental companies.[5]

CRSs certainly benefit everybody involved: the airlines, the travel agents, and the passengers. They can avail themselves of a great number of diversified services, and they can do this without delay caused by busy telephone lines and the like. CRSs also serve many other purposes, among

1. *See infra*, Annex A, p. 80/81, IATA, Guide to Automation, definition of 'system'.
2. Ott, Commercial Aviation, p. 68.
3. CRT = Cathode Ray Tube, i.e. screens; figures from: *Travel Weekly*, February 23, 1987, p. 39.
4. Sabre is used here as an example only because its figures are the most impressive ones as Sabre is the largest system by virtually any measure.
5. Fahy, Regulation, p. 232.

1

them are airline marketing and office management for travel agencies. It appears that 'the sky is the limit' for future developments.

For all their advantages CRSs have become an extremely important marketing tool for the carriers. This obviously means that system failures can cause very serious trouble for the operations of participating airlines, travel agents, and for affected passengers.

Given their importance CRSs can afford their operators substantial market power, too. According to a 1983 U.S. Department of Justice investigation travel agencies accounted for about 60% of all airline bookings and nearly 90% of all agency-booked revenue came from automated agencies.[6] These figures are likely to be higher today. This means that those carriers which do no operate a CRS ('have-nots') are highly dependent on having their schedules, fares and seat availabilities displayed in the systems of the vendors of these systems and of being offered the opportunity of reservations being made through the CRSs. How important it is for any airline to have its services displayed in the available CRSs was evidenced by a move of People Express Inc. in the fall of 1986. In order to facilitate relations with the travel agency community and as a part of an overall strategy to increase its share of the corporate travel market, People Express entered the computer reservations systems of United Airlines, American Airlines, TWA, Eastern Airlines and Delta.[7] This dependence gives the vendors a certain degree of power over their competitors. The use of this power by developing biased software and employing other means, in order to favour the vendors' air services over their competitors' resulted in the adoption of rules by the CAB in 1984 which were supposed to stop competitive abuses and consumer injury.

As the American market now has reached a high degree of saturation U.S. vendors of CRSs develop a taste for the European market. Originally there used to be only one CRS in practically any of the European countries. Competition by U.S. vendors is likely to cause major repercussions. As a matter of fact, the mere threat has already resulted in European activities.

The U.S. experience and the European situation make it worthwhile to study the options policymakers have in regard to CRSs. This study's objective is to determine which policy would optimize the passenger's situation in regard to CRSs. The degree of organization of passengers is lower than that of airlines or travel agents. Passengers' positions are voiced less frequently than airlines' for example. This is probably the reason why the passengers' benefits appear sometimes to be somewhat neglected in the discussion of CRSs. While this study shall be objective and impartial it will

6. *See* U.S. Department of Justice, *1985 Report*, p. 7.
7. *Business Travel News*, September 15, 1986, p. 37.

2

be undertaken with a particular interest to find out which policy option with respect to CRSs could serve the passengers best. A separate chapter will briefly discuss the transborder data flow implications of CRSs.

The volatile situation in the CRS industry where the introduction of amazing new capabilities can happen at any time and where commercial decisions keep changing the situation constantly makes specific statements about technology or corporate structures outdated very quickly. Thus it is impossible to give an account of permanent validity. The descriptive parts of this work therefore are meant to exemplify the trends and developments in this field which is characterized by never ceasing change.

As this study focuses on the policy options to remedy certain problems there will be much emphasis on the factual conditions, particularly because there is very little scholarly writing on the subject.

CHAPTER I

THE STATE OF THE INDUSTRY

In this chapter several of the CRSs presently marketed will be described. The selection of systems is due to the information available to the author and does not allow any inferences as to the market shares of the respective systems, their level of technology and the like (unless expressly stated). However, some of the systems described below have certainly a significant position in the industry.

A. NORTH-AMERICAN SYSTEMS

I. SABRE – AMERICAN AIRLINES

Sabre[1] is the CRS of American Airlines and the world's largest system by any standard. According to a statement by Robert Crandall, the chairman of American Airlines' parent company AMR, made in 1986, 46% of industry revenue and 40% of the automated bookings go through Sabre.[2] The system came on line as an in-house system in 1964 and was offered directly to travel agents after an attempt to produce an industry reservation system had failed in the 70's because United Airlines had started offering its Apollo system.[3] Sabre has 12,000 travel agencies as subscribers, i.e. more than a third of the U.S. automated agencies.[4] These agencies have about 50,000 terminals.[5] Sabre was operational in about 100 travel agency

---

1. The acronym originally stands for 'semi-automated business research environment' – Staar Waars, unpublished presentation by Robert Crandall, Chairman and President, AMR Inc., to clients of First Boston on March 11, 1986.
2. Feldman, CRS Controversy Grows, p. 33.
3. Ibid.
4. *Travel Weekly*, February 23, 1987, p. 39.
5. Ibid. On February 2, 1987 the U.S. Department of Transportation opened an investigation of possible abuse of market power by CRS vendors; the study will, among others,

locations in Europe by the end of 1986.[6] American Airlines recently took delivery of five additional IBM 3090 mainframe computers. In 1986 the airline committed $100 million to develop and expand Sabre, including the construction of an underground base for the central system at Tulsa airport. This 96.000-square-feet centre provides protection against man-made or natural disasters.[7] The Sabre network is able to handle circa 1500 messages per second and to process about 46 million transactions daily.[8]

The American Airlines data network (AADN) is a project launched in 1986; it is designed specifically for Sabre and is supposed 'to pave the way for a worldwide communications network'.[9] AADN uses fibre optics instead of hard cable and links the central Sabre facility with 13 'nodes', or regional sites. In the event of a breakdown in any part of the network, Sabre's data flow will be redirected automatically via alternate circuits. The Sabre system is a direct access system, i.e. a system through which real time direct access to other air carrier sytems is possible.[10]

The Sabre system offers a wide range of information and services specifically designed for certain needs. Weather data in more than 500 U.S. cities and overseas destinations are available[11] and rail services can be accessed through Sabre as well as companies which offer limousines, recreation vehicles, cruises and yachts. Reservations can be made on 11.000 hotel and condominium properties.[12] The core of the system are its airline-related features: schedule information for more that 650 airlines world-wide, more than 25 million air fares, reservations facility for about 300 different carriers.[13]

Apollo's fare information is one of the most important features of the system. The CRS can display fare rules in summary or in full text. It also prices air itineraries automatically. In order to check alternative prices for U.S. travel, the system can check all available fares and rules and quote the lowest possible fare for a planned itinerary. A previously booked itinerary can also be analyzed by the system, which then checks for lower fare availability, and, if needed, provides instructions for rebooking.

A separate product is ADS (Agency Data Systems). ADS provides circa

→ determine the market shares of the individual systems. *Aviation Daily*, February 3, 1987, p. 169/170.
6. Feazel, European Airlines Express Concern, p. 101.
7. *Aviation Daily*, September 23, 1986, p. 470.
8. Shifrin, American's Parent Company, p. 71.
9. *Aviation Daily*, September 23, 1986, p. 470.
10. *See infra*, Annex A, p. 78, IATA, Guide to Automation.
11. *Aviation Daily*, September 4, 1985, p. 9.
12. Fahy, Regulation, p. 232.
13. Ibid.

3000 agencies with computerized accounting, bookkeeping and other business management systems.[14] This line of services is known as a 'back-office system', in distinction from the 'reservation product', the 'front room product'. In 1986 there were a little over 8000 ARC (Airline Reporting Corporation) approved agencies in the U.S. using back-office systems.[15]

Satellite ticket printers allow agents to deliver tickets electronically to a client's premises, without staffing it. In late 1986 Sabre had put out about 100 printers.[16] Commercial Sabre is a user-friendly version of the system designed for the commercial office that wants to make its employees' bookings in-house. 'Eaasy (sic) Sabre' is another user-friendly CRS which is available to users of personal computers. In March 1987 American Airlines began to market a software product designed to allow corporations to monitor employees' travel and entertainment expenses before and after they travel. This new product compares data contained in a personal computer at the corporate site with data it picks up from passenger name records (PNR)[17] in Sabre. The program then can highlight travel that does not meet policies on prices for hotels or cars or class of air service. It shows where the corporation's own negotiated air or other services are not used and reveals such things as which travellers hold more than the permitted amount of travel advances or when too many executives are set to travel on the same aircraft. The programm will also assist corporations in dealing with tax code provisions concerning business expense deductions.[18]

AMR, the parent company of American Airlines, is expanding its data processing and communication sales, both within and outside the airline business. AMR chairman Crandall expects computer services ultimately to provide 25% of the revenue and 40% of the corporation profit.[19] While in the years between 1976 and 1983 there were negative cashflows of about $350 million (the cost of capital included),[20] in 1985 Sabre produced a $142.6 million operating profit. In 1986 American Airlines established a new subsidiary, AMR Information Services (ARMIS). And there are other subsidiaries, too, which provide services to other airlines and other companies which are not in the aviation field.

14. Shifrin, American's Parent Company, p. 77.
15. *Travel Weekly*, September 4, 1986, p. 1, 4.
16. Shifrin, American's Parent Company, p. 77.
17. *See infra*, Annex A, p. 80, IATA, Guide to Automation, for definition.
18. Shifrin, American's Parent Company, p. 77; *Aviation Daily*, March 16, 1987.
19. Feldman, CRS Controvery Grows.
20. Crandall, *supra*, p. 4, note 1.

Apollo is the CRS offered by United Airlines. As many others it evolved from an internal reservations system of the airline to a major operation open to travel agents and other users. It was in place as an in-house system in 1971 after an early computer system in the late 60's had failed to meet demands of high volume.[21] In 1976 Apollo became available to the public.[22] The computer services known as Apollo are actually offered by an affiliate of United Airlines, Covia Corporation. On March 1, 1987 there were 8,650 locations of Apollo in 40 countries[23] (after 7,400 in 1986)[24] with more than 40,000 CRTs.[25] 8,200 of these locations were in the United States and Canada, 250 in Europe and the Middle East, and 200 in the Orient and the South Pacific.[26] The system operates with eight IBM mainframe computers and processes up to 1,300 messages per second.[27] Through Apollo Services a user of the system has access to 653 airlines with 194,000 origin/destination city pairs. The stored information contains over 14,000 hotel properties, 17 car rental companies, 21 tour operators and 13 travel related services companies (including insurance services, railroads, travel information, event tickets, etc.).[28]

A special service, Corporate Apollo[29] provides a travel agent's client with access to Apollo's flight availability and fare and rules information. The client also can make his own air reservation. The data entered by the client will be transmitted to the travel agent for checking and performing of the ticketing. This product lets the travel agent maintain control over ticketing – with the effect that he receives his usual commission – while giving the client some direct access to Apollo – and thus saving time for the agent who shifts a part of his workload to the client.

III. Reservec – Air Canada

Reservec is the name for the CRS operated by Air Canada. This system was first offered to travel agents in Canada in 1973 by giving access to what was

21. Hurley, Mighty Apollo.
22. Ibid.
23. According to a fact sheet 'News about Apollo Services' distributed by Covia Corp.
24. Travel Weekly, February 23, 1987, p. 39.
25. Sturken, Covia Corp., p. 1 col. 4.
26. 'News about Apollo Services', note 23.
27. Ibid.
28. 'News about Apollo Services', note 23.
29. See 'Corporate Apollo' – sales material distributed by United Airlines.

previously Air Canada's internal reservations system. In 1984 approximately 90% of the 3,000 appointed agencies in Canada had become automated. Reservec installations at that time represented 87% of the market.[30] Now there are more than 3,500 automated travel agencies[31] and Reservec retains close to three fourths of all installations,[32] with about 15,000 terminals.[33] The average volume of transactions is three million a day.[34] The core of Reservec is a service called 'Airline', i.e. the airline reservations system. 17 airlines manage their seat inventory through this service, allowing bookings on a 'last seat availability' basis. 'Airline' contains information on fares, schedules, and connecting flights for 47 other international carriers with bookings obtained on a basis of seat availability with updates by the supplier airlines. This means that on these airlines reservations can be made only as long as the flight is 'open'; the flight will be closed when there are a couple of seats left which then cannot be booked through Reservec. Automatic pricing is available, even though not for all flights listed. Reservec further contains information regarding non-participating carriers as available in airline guides.

Another service within Reservec is 'Hoteline', giving access to 3,000 hotels worldwide with various display options according to chain, rate, corporate rate and area. Through 'Autoline' 13 car rental companies can be booked worldwide; a 'bargain shopper' function allows to compare the prices at which a specific make and model of car available in a particular location is offered by various companies.

Tours can be booked on Reservec, as can be Canadian and European railway tickets, ferries, cruises, and theatre tickets in Toronto, London, Paris, New York and Las Vegas. Travellers cheques and insurance are available through this CRS.

Passenger Name Records (PNRs) contain information concerning arrangements made for a travel agent's client through Reservec. For frequent travellers an agent can build up data bases which store relevant data that might be needed on later occasions. Reservec allows for electronic mail to be transmitted to other agencies. Where an agency has branch offices it is offered 'interoffice' mutual access. Travel information in the broadest sense is kept in the Display Reference Information (DRI), an electronic 'library'.

---

30. According to a letter dated June 21, 1985 from the chairman of the Canadian Joint Government Industry Task Force Computer Reservation Systems, Anne-Marie Trahan to the Canadian Minister of Transport, The Honourable Don Mazankowski, P.C., M.P., referring to a CP Air source.
31. *The Gazette* (Montréal), April 28, 1987, business section.
32. *Travel Weekly*, February 2, 1987, p. 1.
33. Roy, Reservec II, p. 84.
34. Ibid.

Reservec further offers a 'queue', enabling the agency to list a number of items which await action. The Reservec hardware meets specific Canadian needs, e.g. with a printer that produces itineraries and invoices in English and French. Satellite printers can be installed in a client's office where they print tickets, itineraries, and invoices which have been processed by the agency.[35]

On April 27, 1987 Air Canada and Canadian Airlines International announced that they would merge the two Canadian CRSs, Reservec and Pegasus. A new company owned 50-50 by the two carriers has been set up to develop the system. The federal Department of Consumer and Corporate Affairs is presently studying the possible anti-competitive implications of the Reservec-Pegasus combine.

B. EUROPEAN SYSTEMS

Below some facts about several European systems will be relayed. In many instances information is based on personal interviews made during a visit to the respective companies. Unfortunately, in some cases interviews could not be arranged so that only a comparatively small number of European systems can be described here. Also written information on the various systems was not always available. The order of presentation is fortuitous.

I. Saphir-Sabena[36]

Saphir which stands for 'Sabena automated passenger hotel integrated reservation' is Sabena's CRS. It came into existence in 1973. Saphir uses the computer facilities of the French Alpha III system operated by Air France. Along with Sabena there are several other (primarily African) carriers which use Alpha III for their respective distribution systems. Sabena pays for the use of Alpha III by certain payments per passenger transported. Approximately one third of IATA approved travel agents in Belgium are equipped with Saphir sets. This means that there are about 100 agency locations of Saphir. 35 of these 100 agencies have ticket printers. These 35 agencies produce approximately 75 % of all Sabena sales. The agencies not equipped

---

35. All information on Reservec was provided by Air Canada in an interview with Ms. Linda J. Eunson (Manager, Computer/Communications Marketing Reservec) on May 7, 1987 and taken from Reservec sales material: 'The New Reservec: Growing Your Way'.
36. Information based on a interview with R. Timmermans, System Reservation Coordination Manager of Sabena, held in Brussels, June 18, 1987.

with Saphir sets most probably cannot afford the rental fees for the equipment.

Even though Sabena does not make any profits with Saphir it still attempts to keep American CRS vendors out of Belgium. In several instances American vendors have in the past installed sets of their systems in Belgian agencies. The installations usually did not result in any costs for the agencies which ordinarily had them installed in addition to their Saphir sets. In response to this development the rental fees for Saphir were recently cut by 50%. In addition plans are being considered to develop the system in order to make it more attractive for agents. Sabena is well aware of the improvements the agents desire: the inclusion of railway services, the development of back-office functions (mainly the production of invoices by Saphir) and possibly the addition of tour operators. However, as Saphir uses the Alpha III facilities every enhancement has to be agreed upon with Air France – a process which is time consuming. Sabena also foresees that at some point terminals might be installed in corporate premises, too, even though these terminals could be used for informatory purposes only and not to make reservations. Sabena also has a policy in place to pay certain overrides. But as these overrides are not based on sales generated through Saphir only they do not support the objective to prevent further inroads of American systems into Belgium.

II. TRAVICOM[37]

Travicom was formed in 1976 to provide a multiple access airline reservations service to UK travel agents. Today British Airways and British Caledonian are the owners of Travicom with shares of 82% and 18% respectively. Travicom is installed in approximately 1,200 locations ('Executive' system) with circa 3,100 terminals. The travel agent presently pays 1,200 British Pounds per location yearly. Travicom employs a staff of 320 out of which 100 are engaged in research and development. Last year Travicom made a profit of 1 million British Pounds on a turnover of 12 to 13 million British Pounds.

37. The following is partially based on information obtained in an interview with Trevor Heley, U.K. Marketing Manager of Travicom, and John Weeks, Marketing Manager Distribution Systems of British Airways, held in Hounslow (Heathrow Airport), England on June 26, 1987, and an interview with Dan Brewin, Senior General Manager Commercial of British Caledonian, held in Crawley (Gatwick Airport), England, on June 25, 1987. In addition sales materials provided by Travicom were used: 'Travicom – The Travicom Reservations System in UK' (issue 3, May 1986) and 'Travicom. A World Leader in Travel Automation Systems' (issued 1 May 1987).

The Travicom system itself does not hold such information as airline flight records of passengers booking details. It rather connects the travel agent's terminal to the computer system of one of the airlines or other providers of travel related services that are participating in Travicom (these participating companies are called 'principals'). To which of the principals the user of Travicom will be connected depends on the user's selection. The particular principal's system then determines the information which is available to users, and the range of transactions which they can carry out. Therefore Travicom in essence is a communications system and a switch.

Travicom, however, performs more functions than linking users' terminals to any of a number of different principals' systems. Travicom acts as a translator of inputs made by the user and of responses as the data pass through the Travicom system. Because the individual principals' systems often require input to be made in a specific format (otherwise the system will respond with an error message) the user without the Travicom translation feature would have to remember the specific requirements of each and every principal. Travicom therefore provides for standardised transactions. This is what a user sees and learns. This standardised transaction will be translated by Travicom into the format expected by the system selected by the user.

The Travicom system is also capable of translating the outputs generated by the principals' systems. Thereby standard forms of display may be created leaving the user unaware of any differences between the various systems which can be accessed through Travicom.

Travicom also is capable of enhancing the principals' systems by adding functions which those systems themselves may not be able to support. For example Travicom can issue tickets from the booking records in any of the airline systems which the travel agent can access, even though some of those systems do not themselves provide an automated ticketing capability.

Travicom further permits interconnection between the Travicom terminal equipment in a user's office and other local data processing equipment which he may use, usually for accounting or record-keeping purposes.

Travicom offers two different reservations systems, 'Executive' and 'Skytrack'. Executive is designed for the large volume business travel agent and allows 24-hour high speed access to the reservations and information facilities of all the principals within the Travicom system. The principals include over 40 carriers, care hire companies, hotels, ABC electronic guide and British Rail. The Travicom neutral airline ticket printer can be linked to the system to provide automatic ticketing. Skytrack provides a videotex link to the main computers of most of the Travicom airlines. The user can receive availability displays and confirmations of bookings. Skytrack is a 'user-friendly' but slower reservations system.

Travicom also offers agency management systems, called 'President' services. These services are back-office functions. 'President Agency Information Systems' allows the agent to use the Travicom database to store his agency's own private pages, to compile client profiles and to send and to receive messages via electronic mail within the Travicom network. 'President Agency Management Systems' provide the agency with automated ticketing, invoice and itinerary printouts and bank settlement plan and management reports. A full accounting system is available, too. These facilities are carried out on the Travicom central computer or locally on IBM personal computers.

Travicom also transgressed the U.K. borders. Among others it established an independent Travicom system in Belgium and started a cooperation in Hongkong. In April 1987 Travicom was reported to have placed a reservation set for the first time with a U.S. travel agency.[38] In March 1987 Travicom and Delta announced an agreement in principle to give subscribers to Datas II (Delta's CRS) a direct access link to Travicom and its principals. In turn, it was expected that Travicom agents will have access to some of Datas II's information packages on hotels, cars and domestic fares. The implementation was projected for the end of 1987.[39]

III. OTHER SYSTEMS

Start is one of two German CRSs, owned by Lufthanse German Airlines, TUI – a tour operator – and Deutsche Bundesbahn – the federal German railway – with a share of 25% each and ABR, DER and Hapag Lloyd – travel agency chains and tour operators – with a share of 8 1/3% each. The second CRS is owned by LTU, Düsseldorf, a charter carrier. Start is conceptually a multi-access system; however, with respect to airline services it gives only access to the Lufthansa system. Start is in place in the vast majority of approximately 1300 IATA approved agency locations in West Germany.

Esterel is a French company which was set up in 1982. Air France, Air Inter and other vendors of transport or tourism services hold an interest in the company. Esterel is a multi-access system, giving access to various reservations systems, including those of air carriers (Alpha 3 for Air France). The system is currently installed in circa 1,300 locations.

In Scandinavia, the dominant CRS is SMART (Scandinavian Multi Access Reservation and Ticketing System). SAS with its RES-AID system and 15

38. *Business Travel News*, April 13, 1987.
39. *Travel Weekly*, March 12, 1987.

other airlines are accessible through SMART. SAS owns 75% of SMART, SJ (the Swedish State Railways) and Branthens SAFE own 12.5% each.

C. ABC – WORLD AIRWAYS GUIDE[40]

ABC International was founded in 1853 as a publisher of railway timetables. Today it is a division of Reed Telepublishing Ltd. ABC International provides the travel industry with information products (such as the World Airways Guide) and other services.

The World Airways Guide contains data supplied by the airlines and gives flight and ancillary information. It has been published for over forty years and is issued on a monthly basis in approximately 86,000 copies. One third of these copies is sold to airlines, one third to travel agents, and one third to other clients, mainly business clients. The market areas for the World Airways Guide are Europe with approximately 36,000 sold copies (95%-98% of the European market), the Far East, Africa and South America. North America is dominated by a similar product, the OAG, published in Chicago.

In the early 1980's ABC undertook a strategic study. The result of this study was the finding that the printed version of the World Airways Guide would not be able to cope with increasingly frequent changes of schedules and fares in a more and more deregulated environment. ABC therefore introduced an electronic version, which in the beginning was the 'book on screen'. The electronic version was improved and nowadays also contains information on hotel accommodations. However, reservations cannot be made through ABC Electronic. ABC does not want to change the distribution system and it is aware of the fact that it would not be able to finance the necessary investments in order to compete in the travel agents' sector. ABC is rather interested to build a system for endusers: in April 1987 it started a booking system in Norway as a pilot project. This project is undertaken on a broader scale and allows hotel bookings, too.

40. The following is based on an interview with Martin J. Nathan, Director-Europe of ABC-Electronic, and Ronald J.L. Speirs, Publishing Director – World Airways Guide, Air Cargo Guide of ABC-International. The interview took place on June 25, 1987 in Dunstable near London, England.

CHAPTER II

WHERE DO CRSs GO TECHNICALLY –
FUTURE ENHANCEMENTS

The development of CRSs never ceases. While even smaller airlines spend millions of dollars on hardware and software[1] every year, the implementation of a major program such as United Airlines' new reservations system[2] may be a $1-billion venture.[3]

There are two basic types of system enhancements: first, the mere extension of a system by linking the CRS to more databases and giving access to other systems. Secondly, the introduction of more complex new system capabilities, such as the integration of front-office reservations and ticketing functions with back-office accounting and management reporting operations or the creation of a computer link between the travel agents and their corporate clients. These enhancements often involve the development of both new software and new hardware.

A. EXTENSION OF SYSTEMS

Of foremost importance in this respect are any improvements with respect to airline services. Therefore more and more links are established between CRSs themselves. American Airlines for instance announced in July 1986 that it would link its CRS with All Nippon Airways within six to eight months, thus creating the opportunity to market the Sabre system to travel agents at more than 1,700 locations in Japan.[4] Since this link is a mutual direct-access link it gives Sabre agents access to All Nippon Airways' Resana

1. *See* the 'Airline Computer Inventory' in Henderson, CRS Vendors Target Travel Agents, pp. 48 et seq.
2. Originally called Enterprise – a name which had to be given up for trademark difficulties, *Travel Weekly*, April 13, 1987, p. 2 col. 1.
3. Author unknown, United to Implement $1-Billion system.
4. *Aviation Daily*, July 28, 1986, p. 148.

14

system.[5] United Airlines while also 'talking with any number of carriers' about such linkups, according to vice president for Apollo services Barry Kotar, generally prefers to have its system directly in place with foreign agents to multi- or direct-access options.[6] United Airlines, however, has agreed to participate, along with several other U.S. airlines, in Multi Japan, a multi-access feature for Japan Airlines' (JAL) Jalcom System. This arrangement is not reciprocal, though, and only allows uses of JAL's system to access the systems of the participating foreign airlines.[7] Other extensions of CRSs may include data bases of non-airline operators, such as the National Tourism Data Base (NTDB), a project of the U.S. Conference of Mayors and United Airlines' Apollo Services. American Airlines also added this data base to its Sabre System.[8] NTDB provides updated information on museums, the performing arts, sporting events, concerts etc. in major metropolitan areas of the U.S. CRS operators constantly expand their connections to ever more hotel and rental car chains, railroad companies, tour operators, cruise ship companies, insurance companies, foreign exchange services, vendors of theater and other entertainment tickets. Often these links not only offer the opportunity to obtain information about the respective services but make confirmed reservations possible, too.

B. INTRODUCTION OF NEW CAPABILITIES

There are more fundamental enhancements than the mere establishment of a link to another database. These more farreaching improvements sometimes only require minor changes of the software, sometimes they practically replace the whole CRS by a new one.

I. EXTENSION OF SEARCH TIME, AUTOMATIC PRICING

An enhancement accomplished by a comparatively simple software alteration may be the extension of the period of time for which a CRS searches for a flight after a request for a certain departure time. Delta for instance enhanced its Datas II CRS in 1986 by giving it the power to programmatically search six hours on either side of the time input for direct international flights.[9] Another interesting new capability is a CRS's pos-

5. *Travel Weekly*, August 4, 1986, pp. 1, 37.
6. Ibid.
7. Ibid.
8. *Aviation Daily*, May 16, 1985.
9. *Aviation Daily*, April 23, 1986.

15

sibility to automatically price a given itinerary. Delta Airlines for example expanded the itinerary pricing capabilities of its Datas II system in 1986. The system now permits computations for double connections and two-stop excursion fares, as well as 'open-jaw' fares for those passengers whose flight ends at one city but begins again at another city.[10] Sabre in 1986 was testing a new product, called Complex International Pricing, which will allow someone to automatically price an international itinerary of up to 24 segments.

II. SECOND GENERATION RESERVATIONS SYSTEMS

Besides separate, comparatively minor enhancements of existing CRSs there are also plans for reservation systems that completely replace existing ones. They ordinarily comprise numerous new capabilities and will often be installed as a 'Local Area Network' (LAN). This network links several workstations together and gives the ability to communicate with other systems as well as to share printers, data and software packages.

a. Focalpoint of Covia Corporation

'Focalpoint' is one of these second generation systems. In April 1987, United Airlines' affiliate, Covia Corporation began testing it. Covia expects to install Focalpoint in 75% of its agency locations within five years. The idea behind this product is to give management more control over the sales process and over client adherence to corporate travel policies. The system is designed to take advantage of recent developments in hardware technology, using IBM's new personal computers (IBM Personal System 2). This is hoped to speed productivity by as much as 25%. The new machines allow to divide the screen of the terminal into four partitions ('flexible windows'). This feature gives the agent the possibility to ask for a client's profile of personal preferences and his employer's corporate policies and simultaneously display in other 'windows' information on availability and fares. The new system further permits digitized travel brochures. These travel brochures are stored on disks and enable the agent to display on the terminal's screen colour photos of particular destinations, attractions or properties.

Management control can be achieved by the use of locally stored scripts that direct staff to take specific steps when selling. For example, a manager

10. *Aviation Daily*, April 1, 1986, p. 5.

can program a script to literally stop the booking process if the counselor does not ask if the client needs a hotel or car booking. Similarly corporate travel policies can be enforced by using the scripting option. Focalpoint also requires fewer keystrokes to complete the same functions. In one example illustrated for the press, a reservation that would ordinarily take 132 strokes using Apollo (the present CRS) can be executed in 52 with Focalpoint.

Focalpoint also includes functions which are known as desktop functions: word processing, calendar, calculator, notepad, clock. Telephone management is also part of the system with telephone directory, speed dialing and automatic redialing.[11]

b. Delta Star of Delta

Delta Airlines began to install a system called Delta Star on a test basis in March 1987.[12] This innovation is supposed to help Delta to achieve a position among the top three U.S. vendors. Delta is currently the smallest of the five U.S. airlines operating CRSs.[13]

The new system's hardware is an intra-office network of IBM personal computers. The set up permits travel counselors to share access to software and a range of locally stored data, as well as to communicate with Datas II, Delta's reservations system. The system will be available in several 'modes'. These modes allow to monitor adherence to corporate travel policies at corporate sites as well as in the agency, they permit cross-checking of proposed travel arrangements with personel travel preferences, and they include a video feature, acting as an electronic brochure by displaying images and information on a particular destination or property. At a later date, 'Easy Reservations', another mode will be made available. This feature will allow an untrained agent to begin selling travel immediately, guided by a series of menu choices and prompts. The transactions then will go into a special file for review before actual ticketing takes place.

III. BACK-OFFICE AUTOMATION

Of great significance with respect to system enhancements is the introduction of 'back-office' automation with accounting, bookkeeping, and re-

---

11. Information on Focalpoint from: Sturken, Covia Corp.
12. *Aviation Daily*, April 3, 1987, p. 20.
13. With approximately 3,100 locations, *Aviation Daily*, April 3, 1987, p. 20; *Travel Weekly*, February 23, 1987, p. 39.

lated management functions. These back-office systems are in the process of being integrated with the front-office systems, i.e. the reservations systems.[14] According to a survey made in 1986 nearly 29% of all U.S. retailers had purchased in-house computers to perform back-office functions (after 25% a year earlier). The American Airlines subsidiary Agency Data Systems was the leading vendor with 3,000 installations. Datas Link (Delta's subsidiary) was second with 800, followed by United Airlines' Apollo Business Systems with 745 installations.[15]

While the CRS of American Airlines, Sabre, and its back-office system (ADS) are still two separate products, data from tickets issued through Sabre can be transmitted to an agent's ADS accounting system for the purpose of collecting information to send out bills and to build management information.

Delta in June 1986 was reported to begin offering an integrated database to travel agents that gives Datas II computer reservations systems subscribers the capability to produce airline reports and management reports on the same terminal where reservations and accounting functions are performed. Called Datas Plus, the system is targeted for agencies that gross $1 million or less in annual revenue, encompassing about 70% of all agencies. This new software was offered as an option at no cost.[16]

The objective to integrate frontroom and backroom operations is the driving force, too, behind a project of United Airlines originally known as 'Enterprise'.[17] The system is planned to be deployed in early 1988.[18] Enterprise will allow to integrate customer travel policies and individual preferences with the travel agent's own policies and product availability. The system can monitor both employee and account productivity, it can track commissions by various criteria for different purposes. Enterprise can produce numerous documents like graphics, cash flow projections, etc. It is also capable of planning, monitoring and evaluating expenses, sales, income, individual and overall productivity levels, etc.

Enterprise also can serve various functions concerning the sales and production management. It can structure the sales transaction at the travel counselor level and thus provide guidance. It can prepare reports for the

14. *See* statement of Terell B. Jones, American Airlines' assistant vice president, Sabre-ADS product development; in: Shifrin, American's Parent Company, p. 77, col. 1.
15. *Travel Weekly*, September 4, 1986, pp. 1, 4.
16. Aviation Daily, June 2, 1986. In February 1987 Delta announced a new back office system for large agencies, called Datasfax, to be introduced generally in fall 1987, *Travel Weekly*, February 23, 1987, p. 39-40.
17. A name that caused trademark difficulties according to *Travel Weekly*, April 13, 1987, p. 2 col. 1.
18. With a delay of nearly two years, *Aviation Daily*, March 25, 1987, p. 446.

customer and documents such as tickets, itineraries, invoices, vouchers, charge forms, custom designed sales documents, etc. The system further allows direct communication with other systems, e.g., customers, subscription services, other travel professionals. Several capabilities of Enterprise are designated as office management functions: electronic mail within the travel agent's system or outside, task scheduling, quality assurance (by creating and monitoring operational standards), various operating levels to accommodate various skill levels, system security (by access control), word processing, human resource management, payroll, operating reports, office budgets, cost control. The system also will allow to establish financial management systems and procedures to meet the agent's specific needs.[19]

C. HARDWARE DEVELOPMENTS

Some remarkable progress has been made by improving the hardware. Apollo document printers produce a new automated ticket and boarding pass with a magnetic stripe on the back. The stripe contains passenger information and a 'mini-itinerary' with air, car rental and travel information. Plans are being made for the ticket to be inserted into a scanner to check in. The passenger will be able to go directly to the airplane. The information will be sent to the car rental company and the hotel thus giving them notice of a delay of the passenger's flight.[20] In the near future, the document printer shall also provide other travel documents, such as car and hotel confirmations and event ticketing. A similar technology is being tested within the Association of European Airlines (AEA): Air France, British Airways, Lufthansa and Swissair developed an ATB (Automated Ticket and Boarding Pass) with magnetic reading.[21]

Delta foresees the possibility of a portable version of its CRS.[22] This would let sales personnel carry terminals to conventions or other events.

Satellite printers already started to extend the travel agent's business into his customer's premises. Air Canada announced the availability of satellite printers for November 1986. The operation of a satellite printer requires the installation of a personal computer in the agency and of a ticket printer in the client's premises. This basic combination costs nearly Can. $900 with

---

19. *Source* of information: Enterprise, sales material distributed by United Airlines, 1986.
20. *Aviation Daily*, March 25, 1987, p. 446.
21. *Source:* Distribution and Automation Challenges, a presentation given by Air France during the 9th UFTAA Automation seminar in Nice, France, April 13-15, 1987. This paper was not published.
22. *Aviation Daily*, April 3, 1987, p. 20.

slightly higher prices for printers that can print itineraries, too, or boarding passes. The booking and ticketing is done through Air Canada's Reservec CRS, with the transmission going into the personal computer in the travel agency. From the agency the information goes to the satellite printer where the ticket, the boarding pass or the itinerary will be printed out.[23] American Airlines had put out 100 satellite printers in November 1986 and expected that number to increase.[24]

The growth potential for satellite printers appears to differ substantially from one CRS vendor to another. When Air Canada began taking orders for satellite printers an airline official said that there was no indication that the machines were going to be in big demand.[25] A vice president of the Airlines Reporting Corporation (ARC) on the other hand in late 1985 anticipated satellite printers to become a popular item. At that time he had just received a request for approval by ARC from one agent who wanted to operate 300 satellites.[26]

Self-service ticket machines were installed by Air France at the Charles de Gaulle airport ('Elise' prototypes).[27] Such machines are also in place in many American airports and in shopping centres. Their use is designed primarily for one-leg shuttle flights and confined to the frequently flying businessman.[28] However, ticket machines are said to offer far greater potential. They could be programmed to interline with other carriers' services and they have the capacity to handle up to eight legs.[29]

A further step might be the ticketless passenger. Socalled smart cards would substitute tickets. Smart cards can hold more information than a magnetic stripe on a ticket: they could be used as a 'mobile passenger profile'.[30] Airlines are now investigating the idea of eliminating the airline ticket. But there are reasons for some reluctance to introduce such a change. One impediment is a legal one: Art. 3 para. 1 of the Warsaw Convention

23. *Travelweek Bulletin*, October 9, 1986, pp. 2, 3.
24. Shifrin, American's Parent Company, p. 77.
25. *Travelweek Bulletin*, October 9, 1986, p. 2.
26. Darbin, Application for Satellites.
27. Distribution and Automation Challenges, unpublished presentation given by Air France during the 9th UFTAA Automation Seminar in Nice, April 13-15, 1987.
28. Renton, Technology Threatens Travel Agents, p. 18; see also: Airlines Investigate Potential of Ticketless Passenger Flights, *Aviation Week & Space Technology*, November 3, 1986, p. 96. Southwest Airlines has begun the sale of tickets through bank automated teller machines in 1986. The tickets were limited to a special $15 one-way stand-by youth fare for travel between Corpus Christi and Houston, *Aviation Week & Space Technology*, November 3, 1986, p. 79.
29. Renton, Technology Threatens Travel Agents, p. 18.
30. Distribution and Automation Challenges, unpublished presentation given by Air France at the 9th UFTAA Automation Seminar in Nice, April 13-15, 1987.

and of the Warsaw Convention as amended at The Hague require the delivery of a passenger ticket containing certain particulars. Art. 3 para. 2 of both versions of the Warsaw Convention provides for the carrier to lose the benefit of the provisions of the Convention which limit his liability if no such ticket has been delivered or if the ticket does not give notice of the applicability of the Warsaw Convention. Only when the Guatemala City Protocol of 1971 enters into force other means (i.e. electronic means) may be substituted for the delivery of a ticket (Art. II of the Guatemala City Protocol of 1971 = art. 3 paras. 2 and 3 of the Warsaw Convention as amended at The Hague, 1955, and at Guatemala City, 1971). Furthermore, passengers feel comfortable having a ticket in their possession, travel agents believe that the ticket is the vital link between them and the airlines (or the passengers for that matter) and the ticket provides the carriers a record to divide ticket revenues among themselves in the case of interlining.[31]

D. HOME COMPUTER LINKS

For operators of CRSs there is a way to get even closer to the passenger than through self-service ticket machines. Home banking systems and other consumer networks could allow CRSs to expand into the consumer's home.

American Airlines' Sabre system already is available in the user-friendly Eaasy Sabre version to subscribers of the General Electric information network for personal computer owners (Geisco) and Compuserve, a similar system. American Airlines also considered to create a joint travel-banking product.[32] In April 1987, it was reported that American Airlines and United Airlines have had discussions with Trintex, a videotex concern owned by Sears Roebuck and IBM.[33] According to this report officials of both airlines said that they had talks with Trintex about supplying Trintex subscribers with the ability to order airline tickets using personal computers. Trintex plans to begin offering shopping, banking and other services to homes in several markets in 1988. Nationwide introduction is scheduled for 1990. But it is not only the private individual who will have direct access to a CRS. The computer manufacturer Data General sells a system called CEO, or Comprehensive Electronic Office, which performs a variety of services, such as filing and budgeting. Commercial Sabre, the corporate version of

---

31. Airlines Investigate Potential of Ticketless Passenger Flights, *Aviation Week & Space Technology*, November 3, 1986, p. 96.
32. *Aviation Daily*, September 26, 1986.
33. *Wall Street Journal*, April 13, 1987.

Eaasy Sabre, was announced to be added to the 'menu' of CEO.[34]

In France, 'Télétel', a videotex system, has meanwhile become a tremendous success: there are 2.5 million terminals, monthly 4,100,000 hours of connection time and over 39 million calls. Télétel offers 4,800 services through its network, many of them from the tourist industry.[35]

There is another trend, too, that brings the consumer and the airlines closer together. Delta Star, Delta Airlines' new CRS version, includes a video feature. The video feature acts as an electronic brochure, using a television monitor to display images and information on a particular destination or property.[36] TWA, too, becomes more involved with information on particular destinations etc. The Travel Channel, a division of TWA Marketing Services, was reported to begin a 24-hour travel-oriented cable television network in February 1987. The programme was planned to be a mix of 50% travel information and entertainment, 30% discount travel offers and 20% direct sale of a broad spectrum of travel-related products.[37]

E. SCENARIO 2000

Considering the developments described above one does not need a great deal of imagination in order to envisage a traveller by the turn of the century (or even earlier): At first he will browse through his electronic travel brochure which he receives as a videotex service. Then he contacts a CRS through his microcomputer at home. He checks fares and schedules or just chooses a programme offered by a tour operator which is stored in the CRS. He makes the flight reservation and several other arrangements, such as the seat selection, rental car reservation and reservation of hotel accommodation. All the necessary information can be stored on his smart card which is a second generation credit card and has substituted the ticket. The passenger will go to the airport on the day of the flight where an automatic check-in takes place, using his smart card again. He will receive computer readable baggage tags and pass automatically through immigration using his computer readable passport. He will board the aircraft using the smart card as a computer readable boarding pass while his bag with the computer readable tag is automatically being routed onto the aircraft. On board there will be a little screen at his seat showing his name and a terminal will inform the flight attendants of preferences or any special care the passenger might need.

34. Ibid.
35. The French Telematics and its Touristic Applicatons, unpublished presentation given by Catherine Rouet (General Directorate for Telecommunications, Télétel Programme Directorate) at the 9th UFTAA Automation Seminar in Nice, April 13-15, 1987.
36. *Aviation Daily*, April 3, 1987, p. 20.
37. *Aviation Daily*, December 12, 1986, p. 387.

CHAPTER III

MAJOR TRENDS AND ISSUES CONCERNING CRSs

In order to identify the benefits passengers derive and the disadvantages they suffer from the operation of CRSs, it is necessary to go beyond a description of the amazing capabilities of the individual systems. Such a description can show the potential automation creates in this field. But this is only a part of the picture. More important is it to find out about the way CRSs are really used in a competitive world, about the government involvement and the experiences made with this involvement, about the role the travel agents play in the distribution chain of the airlines and about the role travel agents are likely to play in the future. In this chapter it shall therefore be attempted to analyze major trends and current issues with respect to CRSs.

A. AMERICAN DEVELOPMENTS

I. THE 1984 CIVIL AERONAUTIC BOARD CRS-RULES

In March 1984 the U.S. Civil Aeronautics Board (CAB) proposed general rules that would forbid air carriers owning CRSs from using their systems to injure consumers and air transportation competition. Comments and reply comments concerning the proposed rules were filed by numerous parties.

On July 27, 1984 the CAB adopted rules on carrier-owned computer reservations systems.[1] They became effective November 14, 1984.[2] The rules are dealing 'with competitive abuses and consumer injury resulting from practices of those airlines that provide computer reservations services

---

1. Included here as Annex B, p 83.
2. Amending 14 CFR Chapter II as a new Part 255.

to other air carriers and travel agents.'³ The rules are of prime importance for this study: here for the first time a government has promulgated regulations concerning CRSs with a view to prevent competitive abuses and consumer injury. The fact that this step was made so early also gives an opportunity to study the experiences made since.

a. The CAB's analysis

The CAB in its notice of proposed rulemaking found that CRS owners have a substantial degree of power over price and output in the CRS industry. This conclusion was upheld despite various challenges to it in the comments filed with the CAB. The conclusion was based on these grounds:

1. Conduct of the CRS owners who could dictate discriminatory fees that were not based on cost, not affected by the prices charged by other vendors and unchanged by pleas that they were excessive; further the owners' forcing other carriers to pay substantial net ticketing fees as a condition of CRS access; further the owners' steadily increasing the degree of bias in their system, with no adverse effect on their CRS market penetration; further the owners' reducing or withholding service on a selective basis to discipline air transportation competitors.

2. Market shares CRS vendors have and the fact that CRSs are in many ways complements, rather than substitutes for one another, with the result that air carriers have little choice but to purchase access to each major CRS in an area it serves.

3. Profits earned by operating CRSs that are far in excess of costs (taking incremental revenues into account).⁴

Another basis for the CAB's rulemaking was the conclusion that CRSs are essential facilities obliging the vendors to afford access to them on reasonable, non-discriminatory terms.⁵

And finally the CAB found consumer injury and consumer deception in the way CRSs were operated and used this as an additional basis for its rulemaking. The CAB concluded that the bias of CRSs causes substantial consumer injury in that it deprives consumers of the opportunity to take advantage of lower fares and causes them to take less convenient flights. And the CAB determined that CRS vendors are engaged in consumer deception because they are parties to agreements establishing travel agents

---

3. U.S. Civil Aeronautics Board, *Regulation ER-1385*, Economic Regulations, Issuance of Part 255, *Docket:* 41686, p. 1.
4. CAB, Regulation ER-1385, p. 3 note 1, pp. 6-15.
5. Ibid., pp. 15-16.

as a common, essentially neutral distribution system. This together with indirect representations that CRSs were unbiased was qualified as a deceptive practive by the CAB because of the existing level of bias.[6]

Appendix – What does CRS bias mean? Bias of a CRS was once defined as 'the inclusion of parameters in software packages to favour the services of the CRS owner and of certain carriers over other carriers'.[7] The bias therefore can be achieved by using a number of factors which are operative when displays are assembled in a CRS. Such a factor may be the individual carrier identity, his nationality etc. Other factors such as 'code-sharing' have also gained notoriety in this respect. However, other methods can be used, too, by CRS vendors in order to manipulate the market. They may refuse to accept a carrier as a participant of the system, they can control marketing information generated through a CRS or include unreasonable contract termination clauses in the agreements with the travel agencies etc.

An excellent account of bias factors and other examples of market manipulation by CRS vendors was presented by the ICAO Secretariat to the Panel of Experts on the Machinery for the Establishment of International Fares and Rates for the 9th meeting of the Panel in Montreal, November 24 to December 5, 1986.[8] This account was included as Appendices 3 and 4 in the Panel's report and is reprinted here as Annex C.

b. The regulatory content of the rules

The CRS rules apply only to systems owned or controlled by airlines and their affiliates because the CAB held that non-airline CRS vendors cannot obtain incremental revenues. Therefore, in the CAB's opinion, non-airline vendors were not inclined to use CRS power to destroy air transportation competition and to injure consumers.[9]

1. The bias rules (Section 255.4)

The rules aiming at the elimination of bias require the provision of a 'primary display' that shall be at least as useful and easy to use as any other display maintained by the system vendor. This was intended to prevent the

6. Ibid., pp. 17-20.
7. CAB, *Report to Congress*, p. 101/73.
8. *ICAO Document FRP/9-WP/2*, 21/10/86.
9. CAB, *Regulation ER-1385*, p. 3 note 1, pp. 20-21.

creation of heavily biased 'secondary displays' which would be more attractive (because of their greater usefulness or easier handling) and therefore turned to automatically by the agents.

The primary displays, to which the CRS rules solely apply, have to contain information that is ordered without the use of factors relating to carrier identity. Sections 255.4(b)(2) and 255.4(c)(3) provide that display selection criteria be disclosed upon request to participating airlines and subscribers.

Also the loading of information has to be performed according to the same standards of care and timeliness for all air carriers and special loading capabilitities (e.g. direct computer-to-computer loading) have to be made available to all participants if offered to any.

2. Contracts with participating carriers (Section 255.5)

After having considered various options regarding the fees participating carriers have to pay (no pricing rule at all, requirement of a reasonable fee level, requirement to offer basic CRS services to air carriers for nothing, i.e. a 'zero fee') the CAB decided to adopt an 'unjust discrimination standard'. This means that discrimination among the carriers in the fees is not allowed, while different fees to carriers based on differences in the cost of serving them is not prohibited.

3. Contracts with subscribers (Section 255.6)

In order to eliminate contract terms clearly designed to prevent travel agents from switching systems the CRS rules limit the length of contracts between vendors and travel agents to five years. The CAB did not include a provision, though, dealing with liquidated damages clauses, i.e. contract clauses under which a travel agent has to make certain payments to the vendor if he should switch systems before the stipulated contract duration is over. The CAB mainly believed that it would be very difficult to devise a liquidated damages formula suitable for all subscriber contracts, given the variety of contracts used.[10]

Other provisions aim at the protection of travel agents' freedom to obtain and to use CRSs instead of or in addition to the ones they use presently.

10. Ibid., pp. 41-42.

4. Other provisions

The CRS rules further require vendors to offer service enhancements to all participating carriers, if they are offered to any (Section 255.7). Also marketing information generated from a CRS shall be made available to all participating carriers on a non-discriminatory basis (Section 255.8).

Exemptions from the application of the CRS rules are provided for those carriers that are unwilling to enter into contracts that comply with the CRS rules or fail to pay non-discriminatory fees (Section 255.9(a)). The system vendor is free to drop such carriers completely from the CRS, to bias displays against such carriers, or to give them equal treatment with paying carriers.

Under Section 255.9(b) the CRS rules also do not apply to a foreign carrier that operates or whose affiliate operates a CRS which is biased against a U.S. carrier.

c. Amendments to the rules

Before the CRS rules became effective the CAB adopted amendments which became effective on November 14, 1984 and November 26, 1984, respectively.

1. Nine connect points requirement

Section 255.4(c)(4)[11] requires vendors that select connect points for use in constructing connecting flights to use at least nine points for each city-pair. This requirement was added because in the CAB's opinion bias in connecting flight displays may be more harmful to air transportation competition and consumers than bias in direct flight displays. The CAB held that connecting flight bias may cause flights to be excluded from CRS displays altogether, while in most cases direct flight bias causes flights to be listed later than they would be absent bias.[12]

2. Disclosure of display criteria to any interested person

Another amendment (Section 255.4(b)(2), (c)(3))[13] concerns the disclosure

---

11. *See infra* Annex B, Part II, p. 87.
12. U.S. Civil Aeronautics Board, *Regulation ER-1395*, Economic Regulations, Amendment No. 2 to Part 255, *Docket:* 41686, p. 2.
13. *See infra* Annex B, Part III, p. 87-88.

of criteria for selection and display of information. This disclosure was originally only required to be made upon request to airlines and subscribers of the systems. However, as the CAB found it to be far less beneficial to the public if not any interested person could request the disclosure of these criteria, it amended the CRS rules accordingly. The CAB identified the following benefits that could be achieved by the amendment: the number of persons monitoring CRS practices would be expanded and the probability of having abuses of CRS power brought to the attention of the monitoring agency would be increased; consumer groups would be permitted to compare the service of the various CRSs, to make recommendations on the best systems, and to enhance public familiarity with these systems so that consumers may better judge the quality of service rendered.[14]

3. Disclosure of international marketing data

The amended Section 255.8 of the rules[15] precludes CRS vendors and participating carriers from releasing marketing, booking and sales data they generate or receive relating to international operations of any carrier, absent authorization to do so. The obligation to distribute marketing information on domestic services extends only to participating U.S. carriers. This provision is intended to strike a suitable balance between the need to protect U.S. carriers from significant disadvantage and the need to ensure basic fairness in dealing with foreign carriers.[16]

II. CHALLENGE OF THE CRS RULES

Petitions of United Airlines, Republic Airlines and British Airways for review of the CRS rules were denied in a U.S. Court of Appeals.[17] The court upheld the CRS rules against challenges of the CAB's rulemaking authority. Also objections to the price discrimination section of the rules were dismissed, as well as an objection against the provision that enables U.S. carriers to employ bias against a foreign airline that operates a CRS that is biased against U.S. carriers.

---

14. U.S. Civil Aeronautics Board, *Regulation ER-1396,* Economic Regulations, Amendment No. 3 to Part 255, *Docket* 41686, p. 2.
15. *See infra* Annex B, Part III, p. 88.
16. U.S. CAB, *Regulation ER-1396, supra* note 14.
17. *Aviation Daily,* July 9, 1985, p. 42.

III. The reaction of the CRS vendors

The CAB's CRS rules rendered all contracts between vendors and participating carriers unenforceable.[18] Therefore the vendors were free to modify their contract terms and fee schedules. The fees charged to the participating carriers after the CRS rules became effective varied from U.S. $0.75 to U.S. $1.85 per booked segment, depending on the CRS involved and the type of service provided (e.g. display of schedules only, display of schedules and bookings on request basis, display of schedules and on-line bookings etc.). This meant a sharp increase in fees for some carriers and a steep decline for others, as fees before the CRS rules ranged from zero in some cases to anywhere between U.S. $0.30 and U.S. $3.00 per booked segment.[19]

IV. Bias after the abolition of bias

As under Section 255.4 of the CRS rules only 'primary displays' were required to be unbiased, CRS vendors immediately introduced 'secondary displays' which were biased against other airlines' services. In these displays, as in the primary displays, closeness of the flight to the requested travel time was the factor which determined the order in which individual services were displayed. However, some vendors treated their own flights as if they were closer to the requested travel time than they actually were. Thus the services of other airlines were displayed as if they were 46 or 60 minutes further away from the requested time than they were in reality.[20]

The vendors went further and created 'lock in' mechanisms, which allowed the agency managers to program the systems so that the (biased) secondary displays came up first and so that the agency employees could not switch to the unbiased primary displays. Because this threatened to render the CRS rules ineffective, Senator Nancy Kassebaum advocated the elimination of secondary displays.[21] American Airlines' chairman Robert Crandall expressed his view that secondary displays violated the spirit of the CRS

---

18. *See* U.S. Civil Aeronautics Board, *Regulation ER-1385, supra*, p. 24, note 3, pp. 39-41. The U.S. Court of Appeals for the District of Columbia has held that the CAB did abrogate prior contracts and that all the old co-host agreements were void: Republic Airlines had filed suit against United that its co-host agreement was not abrogated by the CRS rules, Republic Airlines, Inc. v. United Air Lines Inc., 796 F. 2d 526 (1986).
19. Boberg/Collison, CRSs and Competition, pp. 179-181.
20. Godwin, Documents Show Lines' Priorities.
21. *Aviation Daily*, March 22, 1985.

rules and offered to withdraw them from Sabre if other vendors would do likewise.[22]

The issue was eventually resolved when the three vendors which had biased secondary displays committed themselves to eliminate the biased displays together with the lock-in features.[23]

Other forms of bias are still maintained, even after 'the abolition of bias'.

The fact that most CRSs favour on-line connections over interline routings, even if the interline connection is closer to the requested departure time and even if it has a shorter elapsed time caused some complaints.[24] Certainly it can be maintained that this bias may in fact be based on consumer preferences, if one can show that on-line flights allow an easier transit and that baggage handling is more secure on such flights.[25] But this is not necessarily the case. This example shows that totally unbiased systems are not perceivable. There will always be a flight higher on the screen than others, and this will be called bias at least by those who operate the other services.

While favouring on-line connections over interline connections may already be regarded as consumer injury, because it reduces the probability that a passenger will become aware of those interline connections which are closer to his requested travel time or the flight duration of which is shorter, certainly code-sharing and change of gauge without change of flight number are misleading and contrary to the passenger's interest, as he often will not even have the theoretical opportunity to detect what is hidden behind these practices.

Code-sharing is based on agreements often entered into by national and regional carriers. Under these agreements the two carriers share a single flight designator code for flights of both airlines on routes where they offer connecting services. Thus a connecting flight appears like an on-line connection while in fact it is an interline connection. This results in this connection being accorded screen display priority.[26]

Change of aircraft gauge without change of flight number means that an on-line connection appears as a direct flight notwithstanding the fact that this service includes a change of aircraft or gauge (i.e. the flight continues with a different type of aircraft).

The U.S. DOT adopted a rule requiring code-sharing airlines to notify passengers about the arrangement when bookings are made and provide the

22. Poling, Federal Units Weigh Bias Rules, p. 97.
23. *See* Department of Justice, *1985 Report*, pp. 31-32, with note 45.
24. Department of Justice, *1985 Report*, p. 35.
25. Ibid.
26. As code sharing usually is not available for non-U.S. carriers, it has become an issue in the current talks between ECAC and the U.S. DOT; this will be discussed later.

name of the carrier which will actually be providing the service.[27] However, since this rule applies only in the U.S., non-U.S. passengers usually are not aware of the code-sharing.[28]

Other practices, sometimes referred to as 'screen padding'[29] have the effect of pushing other services further down on the screen or from one screen to a subsequent one, thus reducing the likelihood that this service will be considered by the CRS user. Screen padding can take different forms, including: the inclusion of multiple on-line connections which can sometimes hardly be regarded as reasonable flight options from a consumer perspective; the multiple use of flight numbers by creating a through flight number for an on-line connection involving a change of aircraft or by presenting a code-shared flight twice (once under each of the airline designator codes involved = dual listing)[30]; the inclusion of extensive information, such as the classes of services available.[31]

Another version of misleading bias is the listing of shorter elapsed times than the carrier actually expects to achieve.[32] This practice favours the affected service as it will consequently appear higher on the screen, provided the CRS uses displays criteria (= algorithms) that afford some weight to the elapsed time. Delta in 1986 charged American Airlines to maintain two different schedules, one for internal purposes and another for the CRS. TWA later supported Delta's complaint to DOT.[33] American denied the charges, maintaining compliance with both the spirit and regulation of the CRS rules.[34] It pointed out that 79% of its flights arrived within 15 minutes of schedule, compared to 60% of Delta's. It therefore

27. A DOT study on code-sharing released in August 1986 has found no evidence that regional airlines which share designator codes with larger carriers have a competitive advantage over independent regional carriers. This study, however, was limited to a small sample of markets and strongly contested by the Regional Airline Association, *Aviation Daily*, August 28, 1986.
28. According to Sylvain Denis, Deputy Vice President Tariffs and Industry Affairs of Air France; the author interviewed M. Denis in Paris, June 19, 1987.
29. ECAC submission in connection with the Department of Transportation investigation into the CRS industry, unpublished enclosure to letter EC 9/8.4/20.2 EC 9/8.4/21-288 of 30 April 1987, p. 4.
30. While several carriers, such as US Air, Southwest, American and United, are opposed to dual listing and have asked the U.S. DOT for a rulemaking to ban dual listing, Pan Am supports dual listing. Pan Am maintains that dual listing is necessary to compete in those markets where it has to cooperate with commuter airlines because of its small domestic operation. Without dual listing the identity of one of the two carriers providing the joint service would be eliminated, *Aviation Daily*, May 14, 1986, p. 254,
31. Ibid.
32. Ibid., p. 37-38.
33. *Aviation Daily*, July 8, 1986.
34. *Wall Street Journal*, June 17, 1986, *Aviation Daily*, June 17, 1986, pp. 433-434.

adjusted many of its published schedules to match its competitors'.[35]

From the passenger's perspective it does not appear to be justified that poor on-time performance records result in those ones having a comparatively good record adjusting their schedules in order to match the poor performance of their competitors. Rather those with a poor record should strive for more timeliness or adjust their schedules according to reality.

It is conceivable that not only CRS vendors manipulate their elapsed times, but participants which are hosted in the systems as well. This was evidenced when American Airlines a little later accused Delta Airlines of having listed unrealistically short flight times.[36]

In March 1987, a high ranking DOT official declared that if delays are not reduced by scheduling talks, the DOT may 'go after it through the reservations system'.[37] In fact the DOT has given a Notice of Proposed Rulemaking and solicited public comments on carrier scheduling practices.[38] The DOT proposed three different approaches: changes in the reservations systems, disclosure of on-time performance or the imposition of performance standards.

In July 1987, the U.S. Senate Commerce, Science and Transportation Committee approved a bill requiring airlines to disclose on-time statistics and imposing limited scheduling regulation.

American Airlines recently announced that after August 1, 1987 elapsed times will not have any bearing on the order of flight displays any more. This does not mean that unrealistic elapsed time will disappear from the screens: as long as there are still CRSs that have algorithms that put some weight on elapsed times, there will remain an incentive to publicize schedules that will very often not be met.

V. DOT INVESTIGATION

Following a recommendation made in a report of the U.S. General Accounting Office to Congressional Requesters[39] and a request of the leaders of the House and the U.S. Senate aviation subcommittees the DOT on February 2, 1987 announced that it would investigate airline-owned CRSs and their effect on airline competition. The five airline-vendors, United, American, Eastern, TWA and Delta, were ordered to submit

35. *Aviation Daily*, August 4, 1986, p. 189.
36. *Aviation Daily*, June 23, 1986.
37. Poling, DOT Blames Airlines, p. 41, column 3.
38. *Docket* 44827.
39. GAO/RCED-86-74.

special reports on several issues. The order seeks information on the fees paid by airlines whose flights are displayed on CRSs, the amount of so-called incremental airline revenues CRS owners earn from the systems, market shares, and the prevalence and effect of restrictive clauses in the vendors' contracts with travel agent subscribers. The order was based on section 407(a) of the Federal Aviation Act.[40]

The information ordered to be filed is very comprehensive[41] and comprises such data like the total number of CRT terminals installed at subscriber locations, at host sale outlets, and other locations, as of December 31 of each year from 1980 through 1986; computer tapes listing all subscriber locations by name, address, and ARC number, date of installation, the number of CRTs in use and net segments booked on the vendor and on other airlines in 1985 and 1986; similar tapes listing all agencies participating in the vendor's override and incentive commission plans; complete descriptions of liquidated damages clauses, including payments received; policies and procedures for conversions and buy outs, and statistics on renewals, conversions and cancellations between 1984 and 1986; detailed cost breakdowns on operations, maintenance, wages, and payments, concessions or other benefits provided to domestic travel agencies as part of the inducement to subscribe or remain subscriber etc. etc.

Because of the sensitive character of this information the DOT was asked to provide confidential treatment for many of the submissions. American Airlines in such a request maintained that the information it would submit concerns trade secrets that would inflict substantial competitive harm on American if it became public.[42] Some of the concerns which are the basis for the DOT investigation are also at issue in a law suit which is pending before the U.S. District Court for the Central District of California since November 1984. In this suit, originally eleven airlines[43] claimed that American and United had violated antitrust laws and caused them competitive injury in operating their CRSs. The plaintiffs estimated in the suit that their damages from American's operation of Sabre came to more than $200 million and

40. U.S. Department of Transportation, Office of the Secretary, Washington, D.C., Order 87-2-1, Information Directives Concerning Computer Reservations Systems, *Docket* 44643.
41. Assistant Transportation Secretary for Policy and International Affairs, M. Scocozza, when announcing the upcoming investigation said that the information the department has asked the vendors to provide 'is going to be very expensive for them to put together', Lassiter, Scocozza Details Plans, p. 1.
42. *Aviation Daily*, March 20, 1987, p. 420.
43. The recent industry merger and consolidations, however, have reduced the number of plaintiffs so drastically that Renton/Gaudin, Reserving Judgment, question if the case will proceed to trial, which is scheduled for 1988.

from United's Apollo to more than $150 million. They asked the court to award triple the damages incurred. According to the original complaint the two major CRS vendors are restricting competition in four ways:

1. biased display of flight information;
2. discriminatory and extraordinarily high fees on competing carriers for the booking of their reservations;
3. use of data generated from the CRSs to identify specific travel agents who could be induced or persuaded to divert their business;
4. delay of entry of competing airlines' data into the CRSs.[44]

Later the plaintiffs amended and supplemented their complaint, charging that the two vendors agreed on and imposed booking fees charged to participating airlines, agreed to impose interline ticketing charges, achieved monopoly power in the CRS industry by engaging in illegal practices, and have plans involving the conversion of independent travel agents to franchised dealers who would sell only the tickets of the vendors or other selected or affiliated carriers.[45]

VI. OUTLOOK

At the present moment, it appears that the competition in the CRS industry will continue with full force[46] and that this in combination with the airlines' need to reduce their distribution costs may have a major impact on travel agencies. For Delta Airlines, for example, ticket distribution costs are its third highest operating expense behind labour and fuel. As the operation of CRSs has been recognized as a marketing device of prime importance it remains a focal point of interest for the airlines. But the proportion of travel agents that are automated has nearly reached saturation.[47] This means that new entries into the CRS industry are highly unlikely, particularly because the costs of developing the necessary software and hardware seem to be prohibitive[48] and given the difficulties to convince travel agents of the advantages of converting to a new system.[49]

44. *Aviation Daily*, November 26, 1984, p. 114.
45. *Aviation Daily*, January 2, 1986, p. 3.
46. Delta for example was reported to be heading to a position among the top three vendors – up from position no. 5 as Delta now has the fewest installations of the airline vendors; in order to achieve this Delta would have at least to double its installations, Sturken, Delta Unveils, p. 1.
47. According to the American Society of Travel Agents by 1985 nearly 90 percent of travel agencies were automated, Department of Justice, *1985 Report*, p. 25.
48. Department of Justice, *1985 Report*, p. 27.
49. Nonetheless, there have been attempts to introduce new systems: in 1986 a Connecticut travel agency was announced to create its own airline reservations system and a Las Vegas →

Also the creation of an industry wide booking system, an idea pursued by the NIBS (Neutral Industry Booking System) Interest Group, was eventually abandoned when the NIBS Interest Group dissolved in early 1987. NIBS was initiated with IATA participation in 1985[50] and had originally as many as 32 members (have-nots). The NIBS joint venture considered the acquisition of an existing system rather than the development of a new one. However, the group was weakened considerably by moves of several of its members: Pan Am entered into an agreement with American Airlines,[51] Northwest acquired a 50% share of TWA's Pars Marketing and Pars Services,[52] System One Corp. was established as the CRS of Texas Air/ Eastern Air Lines.

These moves evidence that the competition in the CRS industry will continue through individual alignments, mergers and acquisitions, i.e. by strengthening the existing systems, rather than through the reconciliation of the policies of a large number of airlines.

CRSs could also contribute to the reduction of the airlines' distribution costs, as well as become an important tool when trying to tie the agencies closer to the carriers. Even though the airlines in public deny plans to bypass the agents,[53] the installation of satellite printers in corporate premises, self-service ticket machines in airports, and home computer links to CRSs create the opportunities to do just that. To cut down on the agents' commissions[54] must have a high degree of appeal in an extremely competitive situation. If this circumvention of travel agents will actually happen,[55] this loss of

---

→ company, Universal Reservations System, began operating a CRS, privately owned and independent of any airline, *Aviation Daily*, August 25, 1986, p. 308. It remains to be seen, though, if these operations will ever grow beyond their local significance.

50. Feldman, p. 62.

51. *Aviation Daily*, April 22, 1986.

52. The purchase was approved by the U.S. DOT on December 4, 1986, *Aviaton Daily*, December 5, 1986, p. 345-346.

53. *See*, e.g. the statements of Max Hopper, American Airlines' senior vice president of information systems made at the Focus on Automation Conference in Atlanta in December 1985, Sturken, American Considering Home Computer Link, p. 1.

54. In the U.S., the 17 largest airlines in 1985 paid about 8 percent of their total gross revenues in commissions, double what the airlines paid out on average 10 years earlier, according to the U.S. Air Transport Association (ATA), Renton, Technology Threatens Travel Agents, p. 16.

55. Many factors will become decisive in the carriers' determination if such a move makes commercial sense. An argument which can be raised against the circumvention of travel agents was voiced by M. Buckman, Vice president subscriber automation of American Airlines, in an interview with the author in Dallas, Juli 16, 1987: an important corporate client might have more leverage over a carrier than over a travel agent in negotiations for discounts on air services, because the travel agent can give in only on his commission while the carrier can, in theory, give in on the whole airfare. Thus concessions made to an →

business could become a real threat to the existence of smaller agencies.[56] The larger ones, however, and chains will hardly disappear. Their position in the distribution system seems to be too strong.[57] They could become targets, though, for a conversion to franchised dealers. This has been alleged by the ten non-vendor airlines in their antitrust suit before the U.S. District Court for the Central District of California.[58] The plaintiffs contended that long-range plans of American and United exist, which, if implemented, would deny competing carriers access to much of the ticket distribution system, which would substantially lessen, if not eliminate the plaintiffs ability to compete against American and United.[59]

Such plans may or may not exist, trends are discernible which undermine the travel agents' traditional independence: override commissions, i.e. additional commissions paid after a certain market share objective was met, are an established industry practice. Air Canada for instance in 1987 announced a 30-cent rebate to subscribers for each air segment booked on its Reservec system; this means that an agency booking 500 air segments a month at a Reservec terminal could cover the costs of leasing the unit.[60] Override commissions and other incentives to book certain carriers are a widespread practice in the U.S., too. However, Section 255.6(d) of the CAB's CRS rules expressly prohibits to make the use of a certain CRS a condition for the receipt of any commission for the sale of the vendor's air transportation services. Also the installation of CRS sets as such along with sophisticated back-office features make agents reluctant to consider a switch, given the need for new training and other adjustments after such a switch.

A prominent role in this trend which ties agents closer to their CRS suppliers is played by the 'liquidated damages'-clauses which are found in many vendor-agent agreements. Under liquidated damages clauses CRS vendors are entitled to the amount of the fees the agent would owe over the remaining term of the contract if the contract is cancelled before its agreed expiration.[61]

---

important client could possibly be kept smaller if he has to deal with an agent rather than with the airline directly.

56. C.B. Lyle, ICAO, Air Transport Bureau, in his presentation to the 9th UFTAA Automation Seminar, Nice, April 15, 1987 spoke about the travel agents' fear of 'loss of their livelihood' in connection with the development of home computer reservation services; unpublished presentation, given to the 9th UFTAA Automation Seminar, p. 5.

57. In 1984, 690 agencies (3.6 percent of the total number of 18,690) had a sum over in excess of US $5 million each; these agencies handled 45.5 percent of the total agency volume; Renton, Technology Threatens Travel Agents.

58. *Supra*, pp. 33-34.

59. *Aviation Daily*, January 2, 1986, p. 3.

60. Godwin, Air Canada Sets Rebates, pp. 1, 4.

61. Department of Justice, *1985 Report*, pp. 22-23.

After the imposition of the CRS rules American, United and TWA strengthened these clauses by adding a measure of damages that is based on projected lost booking fees from other carriers over the life of the contract due to the subscriber's booking activity.[62] The U.S. Department of Justice in its 1985 CRS Report calculated that under American's lost booking fee formula a six-CRT agency that is halfway through a five-year contract has to pay US $63,000 alone in lost booking fees, several times the damages due under the former liquidated damages clauses (lost agency fee basis).[63]

Only recently, in March 1987, there was a summary judgment against an agency owner whose firm switched reservations systems at midcontract and failed to pay the fees which became due. This decision of a Texas state court apparently was the first judgment awarding liquidated damages including the booking fees the plaintiff, American Airlines, would have earned from other airlines if the contract had not been terminated before its full term was over. The award of US $232,454 included $100,000 for liquidated damages. The defendant had leased Sabre equipment with four CRTs.[64]

And then there is the 'halo'-effect. This has always favoured the vendors, not only lately. Halo effect simply stands for a predilection on the part of the travel agencies to favour their vendors' air services. A great variety of factors contribute to this effect, not only tangible advantages, but impalpable things, too, such as good personal relationships. All this cannot establish proof that the conversion of travel agencies into dealerships which are offering only a limited range of products really is the airlines' long-term strategy. However, given the current developments the ground gets more and more prepared for such a transformation. And such a transformation might make a lot of commercial sense for the carriers.[65]

B. EUROPEAN DEVELOPMENTS

I. BIAS IN EUROPEAN CRSs AND GOVERNMENTAL ACTIVITIES

No regulations dealing specifically with CRSs have been adopted so far in any European country. This may or may not have its reason in the fact that in many European countries the governments wholly or partially own the

---

62. Ibid., p. 23 with the various lost booking fees formulas under the vendors' liquidated damages clauses. See also: *Aviation Daily*, May 22, 1985, p. 126, June 11, p. 229.
63. Department of Justice, 1985 Report, p. 24.
64. Godwin, Judge Includes Liquidated Damages, pp. 1, 71.
65. Similar views were expressed 'off the record' to the author by several senior IATA officials in interviews in Montréal and Geneva in May/June 1986.

national carrier and therefore do not see a need or do not want to subject airline-vendors to CRS rules. In effect, European CRSs often are more biased than American systems. The more prevalent bias of European systems often is freely admitted by Europeans. Marcel Pisters, Deputy Secretary General of the Association of European Airlines (AEA), for example says that European CRSs undoubtedly are more biased against non-European carriers than vice-versa.[66] An account of bias in European CRSs[67] made by the Associate General Counsel of American Airlines contains the following items: European CRSs store fewer city pairs and therefore may not always show on-line connections on U.S. carriers that the 'hub and spoke' route networks[68] of these carriers allow; European CRSs build connecting flights through fewer connect points and therefore cannot show connecting flights through the various major U.S. hubs; European CRSs display U.S. carriers' services at less favourable positions (lower on the screen or on later screens).

U.S. vendors also complain about the problems they encounter when they try to market their CRSs in Europe. In some places they cannot get communications lines for their systems,[69] and sometimes the participation in Bank Settlement Plans (BSP) which settle the accunts between agencies and airlines is impeded.[70]

In fall 1987 American Airlines commenced a legal action with the EEC as well as in Great Britain. American Airlines considers the fact that British Airlines does not allow the issuing of British Airways' tickets on Sabre of prime importance with respect to its opportunities to compete in Europe. If the British courts or the European Commission were to share American Airlines' view that British Airways' conduct is unlawful, these actions would have a tremendous impact on the European CRS situation.

As stated above, no national legislative actions have been taken so far in order to remedy any grievances. H. Raben, Director-General of Civil Aviation in the Netherlands analyzed the situation and concluded that there are good reasons for the Netherlands government to look closely at the developments in the CRS market. He doubted, though, that national rules

66. In an interview with the author, given on June 18, 1987 in Brussels.
67. Fahy, Regulation, pp. 237-238.
68. I.e. route networks with a hub which is usually located somewhere in the interior of the U.S. and from where many cities can be reached directly. If the hub is at the same time the carrier's gateway to the U.S. for international flights, it allows many destinations to be reached through one connect point (i.e. as a two segments trip).
69. This is a problem, though, that CRS vendors are not experiencing alone, Feldman, The Fight is on, p. 65.
70. Ibid.; Fahy, Regulation, pp. 240-241. Similar complaints were voiced by Henry Feinberg, General Manager – Pacific of United Airlines' affiliate Covia in an interview with the author in Chicago, July 14, 1987.

are the right answer. In his view national legislation might put the Netherlands into a disadvantageous position with regard to countries that do not have any CRS rules in place. He held that international rulemaking is necessary because different rules in different countries will not ensure equal opportunity to compete.[71]

However, CRS issues have been brought up at different bilateral negotiations the U.S. have had with European governments. Complaints of TWA, Northwest and Pan Am concerning the display of their services in the German CRS 'Start' were filed at the U.S. DOT in May 1985[72] and later withdrawn when Lufthansa and the American carriers agreed on an unbiased display in Start in exchange for booking fees from the participating carriers.[73]

In 1986, CRS problems were discussed in Swiss-U.S. bilateral negotiations.[74] In April 1987, the United Kingdom introduced CRS issues in bilateral talks with the United States.[75] And in May 1987 a proposed U.S.-Dutch agreement included some provisions on the operation of CRSs. The proposal would allow CRS vendors of one country to bring their systems into the other country, maintain them there and make them 'freely available' to travel agents of that other country. Under the proposal neither country could impose on the CRS vendors from the other country more stringent requirements than those imposed on its own vendors regarding installation and displays. And airlines designated to provide air transportation under the proposal would have to participate in airline-vendor CRSs in their own country to the same extent that they do in those systems when used in the territory of the other country.[76]

CRS problems have been dealt with on a multilateral basis as well. Following an initiative of the European Civil Aviation Conference (ECAC) CRS issues were included as an agenda item of the tenth ECAC/U.S. meeting on North Atlantic pricing, held in Washington, D.C., 14-17 October 1986.[77] The ECAC delegations pointed out that in their opinion

71. Raben, CRS, pp. 24-25.
72. *Aviation Daily*, May 22, 1985, p. 126.
73. Aviation Daily, March 6, 1986, p. 357; Fahy, Regulation, pp. 239-240 contests that the agreement reached has really had a satisfying effect on the way U.S. carriers' services are displayed in Start.
74. *Aviation Daily*, July 9, 1987.
75. *Aviation Daily*, April 2, 1987.
76. *Aviation Daily*, May 7, 1987.
77. The following is based on information obtained in an interview with Kevin Kealy, Air Transport Officer of ECAC, and David McKnight, Statistics and Systems Officer of ECAC, in Paris, June 19, 1987 and an interview with Cindy Burbank, U.S. Department of Transportation, Office of Policy and International Affairs, held in Washington, D.C., July 15, 1987.

the effect of U.S. CRSs was that ECAC carriers were denied fair and equal opportunity to compete. Use of through flight numbers for services involving a change of aircraft, code-sharing, and screen-padding were the practices on which ECAC concerns focused. The American delegation countered by highlighting what it considered to be an even more effective bias found in European systems. In January 1987 and in July 1987 demonstrations of various systems were given in Washington, D.C. and in Paris. The present 'exploratory phase' might be followed by discussions on a higher level. It remains doubtful, though, if there will be an agreement such as an U.S./ECAC Memorandum of Understanding on CRSs as both sides appear to differ on the importance of this issue.

II. THE VENDORS' ACTIVITIES

There are several reasons why Europe has attracted much attention among those who are either actively involved in CRS activities or are observers of the scene. As the American travel agency industry has reached a high degree of automation, European agencies have become a desirable target for U.S. CRS-vendors. In Europe, the degree of travel-agency automation in general is lower than in the U.S., there is often very little competition as the flag carrier frequently is the only vendor in any given country, European CRSs tend to be less competitive than American systems. As the installation and connection of new CRS sets becomes less costly with the system's growth, the addition of further installations can add new sources of income at only small increases of costs. European airlines, on the other hand, have an interest to keep U.S. CRSs out of their countries: more American CRS installatons in Europe would reduce the European carriers' control over the distribution of their services, it would reduce the revenues of those European vendors who make profit with their systems, and it would increase their distribution costs as they would have to pay booking fees for those services sold through American CRSs. Also travel agencies in Europe are reluctant to install American systems. These systems cannot yet replace the various European CRSs because their databases do not contain all the information a European travel agent needs. However, large agencies with substantial U.S. oriented business have in the past sometimes installed American CRSs because they were interested in the vast information on the American market they could access through a Sabre or Apollo terminal for example. But since this means additional costs for the agent, as well as more training time for his employees and additional space requirements, it can hardly be expected that agencies in large numbers will opt for an American system besides their national CRS.

40

As a matter of fact only relatively few installations of American CRSs in Europe exist. There were for example only 180 agency locations of Sabre in Europe in July 1987 and 100 Apollo locations.[78] Difficulties the U.S. vendors experience with obtaining communications facilities and participation in bank settlement plans may be responsible for this slow motion. But the time the Americans lose while trying to cope with these problems is also used by the European CRS operators in order to catch up with the Americans. Prices are cut,[79] comparatively large investments are made in order to upgrade existing systems or to create new ones,[80] i.e. the threat of the American invasion increases the competitiveness of European systems.

But all these efforts will not suffice because of the scale of investments the American vendors have been able and continue to be able to make. American Airlines will spend another U.S. $1 billion on Sabre over the next five years in addition to the U.S. $3 billion it has already paid to create and develop Sabre.[81] Also United Airlines' new system is a venture in the U.S. $1 billion range.[82] As the European Airlines were aware of their limited capabilities to compete with American vendors individually, they launched a study in order to explore the feasibility of a joint and neutral CRS (Global Distribution System = GDS).[83] The study was commissioned by the Association of European Airlines (AEA) at a cost of $500,000. Only four months later the study was completed. The study's major findings were:
– that a system can be developed which would be competitive with any other system in the world;
– that it is feasible to develop such a system technically, legally, and economically;
– that such a system can be profitable.
The study determined that a holding company with three subsidiaries (for marketing, operations, and development) owned by the airlines should be established. The system itself would consist of a central site computer ('core system') linked to the computer systems of the individual airlines and to the travel agents through national 'gateways'. The study did not say if a GDS was politically feasible.

Several airlines started studying the development of a joint information and reservations system (with fewer participants than a GDS would have)

---

78. *Travel Management Daily*, July 13, 1987.
79. *Supra*, p. 10.
80. Swissair for example is investing about $25 million to upgrade its current system, Feazel, European Airlines Express Concern, p. 103.
81. Ibid., p. 103; Renton/Gaudin, Reserving Judgment, p. 22.
82. *Supra*, pp. 7, 12-14.
83. Information on this study was obtained from Marcel Pisters, Deputy Secretary General of the Association of European Airlines, in an interview held in Brussels, June 18, 1987.

already when the AEA was still evaluating the findings of its feasibility study.[84] After several remarks made by high ranking Lufthansa and Air France executives that a GDS would be ineffecient and a waste of both time and money and that it might be better to work with just three or four airlines,[85] it did not come as a big surprise that in mid-June 1987 Lufthansa, Air France, Iberia and SAS announced a joint CRS project, called Amadeus. Meanwhile the Amadeus group has decided to purchase System One's CRS for its operation. The new system is scheduled to begin operations in 1989. The four carriers said that Amadeus will require an initial investment of approximately $300 million and that it will employ a staff of 550 employees in its first year of operation. The four airlines will hold equal shares in the company, but other European and overseas airlines have been invited to take part in the new system. Amadeus will be run by a holding company based in Madrid. Three companies will be formed under the parent company – a development company headquartered in France, an operating company based in Germany (Munich) and a marketing company based in Madrid. Obviously the Amadeus carriers share the conviction that their project would offer some advantages over a GDS as far as the management of the system is concerned while still meeting their objective to create a CRS that is capable of competing with the large American systems.

Only three weeks later, British Airways, KLM, Swissair and Covia, the vendor of Apollo, announced that they have launched a venture to provide a new CRS for the travel industry in Europe.[86] This group, the Galileo group, is investing $120 million to put their system into the market by early 1988. The carriers, which have meanwhile been joined for example by Alitalia, British Caledonian, and AUA, said that they will pool existing distribution software and communications technology. This move should give United Airlines' affiliate Covia a competitive advantage over American Airlines in Europe. Covia now will have access to the European market without the necessity to create a complex European operation of its own in order to adjust its CRS to the specific European needs. Also any administrative obstacles will most probably be surmounted more easily by this U.S./European joint venture than by an American company alone.

American Airlines had approached the Amadeus group with no success, because this group was not willing to accept American Airlines as a partner, while American Airlines was not interested in merely selling its software. As there are now not many airlines left which are not member of one or the other alignment it is not very likely that American Airlines will get involved

84. Levere, European Lines, p. 1.
85. *See* for example: *Airline Business*, April 1987, p. 8.
86. *Travel Management Daily*, July 13, 1987.

in a European joint venture. However, recent success in marketing Sabre in Europe despite the announcements of Amadeus and Galileo fuels American Airlines' hopes to develop and maintain a significant market presence, anyway. American Airlines considers its success in the Canadian marketplace a precedent in this respect. The fact that only recently American Airlines was admitted to several bank settlement plans is viewed by American Airlines also as an encouragement to further market Sabre in Europe. American Airlines also hopes to obtain help from the EEC with respect to the refusal of several airlines to authorize the issuance of their tickets through Sabre.[87]

C. CANADA

In Canada, a Joint Government-Industry Task Force on Computer Reservations Systems was established in response to a requirement of the air policy issued on 10 May 1984. The main, overall finding of the Task Force which was reported to the Minister of Transport in a letter on 21 June 1985[88] was that neither of the then existing Canadian CRSs, Air Canada's Reservec and CP Air's Pegasus 2000, was operated with a view toward creating a competitive advantage for itself and thereby discriminating against other carriers reliant on their system. The Task Force expressed its belief that, with one exception, the supply of information in Reservec and Pegasus was adequate. The exception was the absence of a display of pricing information that would enable travel agents to advise consumers quickly of the lowest fare offered on a requested routing, without the need to make a number of inquiries. Thus the Task Force only recommended that the Air Canada Board of Directors be asked to take steps to ensure that the Computer and Systems Services Branch of the company, which is responsible for Reservec, continues to be operated as an independent entity, and that Reservec remains free of bias. CP Air according to the Task Force's recommendation should be encouraged to follow the same approach. The Task Force further recommended that both Canadian CRSs proceed with the development of improved programs for the display of pricing information and continue to pay heed to the need for training of travel agents. The Task Force also found that it would be prudent periodically to reexamine the problems and issues

---

87. Information based on a telephone interview with Mike Buckman, Vice President Subscriber Automation of American Airlines, held on September 21, 1987.
88. Unpublished letter by Mme Anne-Marie Trahan, Q.C., Chairman of the Joint Government-Industry Task Force on Computer Reservations Systems to the Honourable Don Mazankowski, P.C., M.P., Minister of Transport.

it investigated, particularly if serious consideration were given to privatizing Air Canada, since privatization and deregulation could encourage CRS owners to begin to use their systems to their own, competitive advantage.

Despite the main finding that neither Canadian system is used for anti-competitive purposes, United Airlines' affiliate Covia Corporation is not convinced that this is true.[89] Covia Corporation is concerned about the fact that Air Canada does not consent to create a direct link between Reservec and American CRSs resulting in the lack of last seat availability information on Air Canada flights in American systems. While Reservec which presently considers to create a direct link with American CRSs denies that last-seat-availability is the decisive feature of a system as far as the marketing opportunities of that system are concerned,[90] Covia maintains that without last-seat-availability its competitiveness in the Canadian market is considerably reduced.

CP Air in a submission to the Canadian Task Force on CRSs had made a similar complaint. However, here the focus was rather on the effect the absence of a direct link had on the expectations that CP Air flights will be booked by Reservec equipped travel agents than on CP's chances to sell its Pegasus CRS. The Task Force came to the conclusion that the benefit to the public accruing from a direct access of CP to Reservec would not justify the disproportionately large benefit CP Air could derive from direct access without having contributed toward the development costs of Reservec.

Covia's complaint is different from CP's in its submission to the Task Force insofar as it is not so much concerned with information regarding United Airlines' services as displayed in Reservec but rather the information regarding Air Canada's services that can be obtained through Apollo and with the opportunity to sell Apollo to Canadian travel agents.

While it is difficult to establish proof for Covia's allegation that Air Canada's denial to create a direct link to Reservec curtails its opportunities to compete, there are figures which show that there is very little competition in the Canadian CRS market from non-Canadian vendors: the Task Force on CRS in 1985 stated in its submission to the Minister of Transport that Sabre and Apollo at that time had a market share of 6 percent and 1 percent respectively. While in 1985 there was still competition from two Canadian vendors for the remainder, after the announced merger of Air Canada's and Canadian Airlines International's[91] CRSs, this infra-Canadian competition

---

89. According to Henry J. Feinberg, General Manager – Pacific of Covia, who was interviewed by the author in Chicago on 14 July 1987.
90. According to Linda J. Eunson, Manager Computer/Communications Marketing of Reservec, interviewed by the author on telephone, July 23, 1987.
91. The product of the merger of CP Airlines and Pacific Western Airlines.

44

will cease to exist. The merger of the two Canadian CRSs was agreed upon despite the fact that the Canadian Transport Commission's decision of February 26, 1987 to approve the takeover of CP Air by Pacific Western Airlines was based in part on Pacific Western's statement 'that it would end its current market alignment with Air Canada to the extent of discontinuing its use of Air Canada's Reservec computer reservations system.'[92]

In the light of these developments a situation that would justify a reexamination of problems and issues connected with CRSs, as recommended by the Task Force on CRSs in 1985, may have occured earlier than the Task Force probably anticipated. Such a reexamination would certainly benefit from the participation of non-Canadian CRS vendors.

D. DEVELOPMENTS IN OTHER REGIONS

The situation in other regions of the world is distinguished by the comparatively low degree of automation, little developed communications facilities,[93] financial troubles in numerous countries, with a few exceptions where the situation can be compared with European conditions. This means that there is little appeal for CRS vendors to market their systems in the majority of countries, while a few states might be promising markets.

Because of a paucity of sources the information given below is limited.

The Orient Airlines Association (OAA) studies the automation issue and watches with concern attempts by Covia and American Airlines to sell their software-packages in the Asia-Pacific market, as there is the feeling that the sold software packages may create an innate bias in the reservations systems, in favour of those airlines who or whose affiliate sold the packages.[94] OAA according to AEA also has approached this organization in order to obtain information on AEA's Global Distribution System project.[95]

At a management seminar for chief executives of African airlines held in Nairobi, under the sponsorship in AFRAA and IATA in 1986, automation issues were discussed. In presentations the following points were made among others:

92. According to an unpublished 'Submission by the Consumers' Association of Canada to the House of Commons Standing Committee on Transport with Respect to the Impact on Airline Deregulation on Air Safety, Airline Concentration, and Privatization', dated June 11, 1987, p. 4.
93. This was stressed as a prime factor by A.D. Groenewege, Director Industry Affairs of IATA, in an interview with the author, held in Geneva, June 16, 1987.
94. TTG Asia, October 17-23, 1986.
95. According to a statement of Marcel Pisters, Deputy Secretary General of AEA, made in an interview with the author in Brussels, June 18, 1987.

- there is a need for a joint approach by African airlines to the future development of automation in the industry, particularly in computerised reservations;
- there is a danger that airlines could lose control of the distribution system to non-airline entrants;
- effective automation systems depend on the availability of reliable telecommunication facilities.

From the discussions, a consensus emerged that AFRAA should pursue further studies of the development of an automation strategy leading to the formulation of a master plan, based on the progress already made by the AFRAA communications sub-committee on the development of a joint reservations system.[96]

96. *African Air Transport*, Last Quarter 1986.

CHAPTER IV

THE PASSENGER'S BENEFITS AND THE PASSENGER'S DISADVANTAGES

A. BENEFITS

The availability of CRSs was instrumental to the U.S. deregulation policy.[1] Without the capabilities of these systems, it would have been exceedingly difficult for travel agents to obtain and to handle the vast amount of information of constantly changing fares and schedules.[2] However, as the question if the passenger actually benefited from deregulation still awaits its conclusive answer, it is not fully clear yet if the fact that CRSs aided deregulation favours the passenger or not.

Similarly, the effect of advanced yield management, which depends on the availability of data generated through a CRS, is an ambiguous one from the passenger's perspective. Yield management aims at increasing the load factor by permanently adjusting the classes of air transportation and the fares to the changes of the market situation. This requires a high degree of intuition as well as the availability of historic and most recent data. While the CRS rules require the airline vendors to make available to all participating carriers on non-discriminatory terms all marketing, booking and sales data that they elect to generate from their systems (section 255.8) the vendors' access to the necessary data is much faster and possible to the very last minute before take-off. And time is of the essence for yield management.[3] The effect of yield management for the passenger has some

---

1. Cf. interview of the *Aviation Daily* with Robert Baker, Vice President – Information Systems of American Airlines, April 10, 1985, pp. 225-226.
2. For the same reason it is fair to say that deregulation has helped automatization of travel agents.
3. A relationship between CRS ownership and an above average load factor was also claimed by Avmark Inc. which in 1986 showed that the load factors of both American Airlines and United Airlines have been considerably higher that the US industry average since 1980, source: *Flight International*, 4 October 1986, p. 5.

ambiguity because at first yield management will result in attractive fares and a higher load factor which may result in reduced prices, too. In the long run, however, if the data required to operate a successful yield management are available only or considerably faster to the CRS vendor, this vendor will further increase its market power with the possibility of domination. This eventually would reduce the passenger's choice.[4]

The ambiguity of these consequences of CRSs notwithstanding, there are also effects of CRSs which appear to be purely beneficial for the traveller: a CRS provides the travel agent with a wide range of information at very high speed. Using the system he is able to save his own as well as his customer's time and money. The travel agent does not need to use unhandy airline guides any more, and he is freed of trying to get in touch with a carrier by using the phone. Also some of the information stored in a CRS may be difficult or time consuming the obtain otherwise (specific information on hotel properties, customs regulations, theatre events in other countries etc.). And the opportunity to book not only air transportation, but also to make reservations for rental cars or hotel rooms, to purchase tickets for a show make all these arrangements very easy. And all this can be achieved at marginal costs. Also shopping for a low fare can be made easy by CRSs: some of them have a feature that allows them to automatically look for the lowest applicable fare for a requested city pair ('bargain-finder' or 'fare-shopper'). All the new technology which keeps being introduced makes things easier, faster, more comfortable or less expensive for the customer. New hardware allows more applications in more locations by more users and with better results. New printers for example print everything from the basic ticket, to the itinerary, the rental car confirmation and the invoices at a very high speed. They can be installed in travel agencies and corporate locations and they can be used by several agents in one agency who just send the data of their transactions to a queue for automatic processing. New software opens a whole world of new capabilities. Again transactions are speeded up by substantially reducing the number of necessary keystrokes. And the adherence to detailed corporate travel policies is being automated, thus facilitating the management of this important sector for agencies and their clients. Frequent flying private individuals profit in a similar way and the availability of CRS services reduces their dependence on the travel agents.

---

4. This concern was expressed by the British National Consumer Council (NCC) in its March 1987 response to the Civil Aviation Authority's consultation paper on safeguards against monopolistic and anti-competitive practices. To the author's knowledge, the NCC's response was not published.

B. DISADVANTAGES

The importance of CRSs and the dimension of some of the systems are the basis for the existing or potential disadvantages that can stem from the operation of CRSs. These disadvantages may work against competitors of the CRS vendor or they may threat the independence of travel agents – almost always they also injure the passenger.

Injury of the passenger may be caused by anti-competitive behaviour of the CRS-airline owner against other airlines. Competitors may be excluded altogether from CRSs by their vendors. Only recently a refusal of Sabena to grant access to its CRS Saphir for London European Airways (LEA) necessitated the intervention of the EEC Commission. LEA operates a Luton-Brussels service since May 1987 at 99 British Pounds for the return flight, i.e. at 40 percent less than Sabena. When Sabena refused LEA access to Saphir because of the potential danger for its passenger traffic and on the grounds that LEA did not intend to grant Sabena the contract for the ground handling servicing of its aircraft, LEA lodged a complaint with the Commission against Sabena for abuse of its dominant position. The Commission started an investigation which was also carried out at the offices of Sabena. When the Directorate-General of Competition notified Sabena of its intention to adopt interim measures obliging Sabena to accept LEA in Saphir, Sabena agreed to the request of LEA to be listed in Saphir.

CRS vendors may also 'merely' treat some carriers on a preferential basis and discriminate against others, even after the adoption of rules such as the CAB's 1984 CRS rules. In some instances, such discriminations may occur inadvertently but the effect is the same: in Apollo for example, the display of the international fares of TWA and other carriers had to be changed after a complaint by TWA that its fares were displayed incorrectly or incompletely while the tariffs of British Airways, Apollo's supplier of transatlantic fares data, were displayed in a correct, timely and accurate fashion. Aer Lingus had a similar complaint: Apollo's display of the Aer Lingus advance purchase basic season fare between Atlanta and Shannon was $1,029, while a comparable British Airways fare of $627 is shown. The correct Aer Lingus fare was $616. These cases stand for a number of similar problems that were not confined to Apollo services; they show that the utmost care of the vendors is called for in order to provide correct information and to avoid consumer injury. And when vendors intentionally favour their own services in their CRS, the concerned question of the chairman of the U.S. House of Representatives Aviation Subcommittee, Representative Norman Minetta is easily answered; Representative Minetta asked: 'Do governments and airlines have the resources and knowledge to nip discriminatory practices in the bud or will CRS vendors always be one step ahead?'.[5]

An anti-competitive effect of the ownership of a CRS may also be achieved by access to the marketing data of other airlines. This allows for very precise price discount competition.[6] In combination with the yield management thus the risk of market domination by the CRS vendors is enhanced. It has still to be determined if section 255.8 of the CAB CRS-rules of 1984 which require CRS vendors to make all marketing, booking and sales data available to all participating carriers on non-discriminatory terms effectively excludes this anti-competitive advantage of the CRS owner. It this is not the case, the CRS owner's advantage will result in the passenger's short term advantage of discount prices and the long term disadvantage of market manipulation by CRS vendors.[7]

Another threat for the passenger resulting from the operation of CRSs is the market dominance CRS vendors may gain from a strong relationship with travel agents. Incentive payments like override commissions and other not necessarily monetary incentives put the travel agent's objectivity under strain.[8] Agents are tied into contracts which provide for substantial liquidated damages if they want to withdraw from the agreements. Even though section 255.6(a) of the CRS rules of the CAB prohibits contracts between vendors and agents for a longer term than five years, it was claimed that actually contracts can run up to 12 or 13 years because the arrival of new equipment at an agency location can mean an extension of the existing contract.[9] CRS vendors compromise other vendors' competitiveness by barring them from participation in bank settlement plans or by not giving them last-seat-availability information about their services, which may substantially reduce the usefulness of a CRS in an area where those services form an important part of the market.

All these individual factors may eventually result in higher prices: higher prices for air services because of reduced competition and market dominance of those airlines that have control of a CRS and higher user fees for CRSs and higher booking fees for the airlines. These higher prices will have to be borne by the person who pays for the ticket as they will all be included in the air fare.

And there is a disadvantage caused by a development which is in its early stages now and which at first glance looks as a straightforward advantage for

5. *Docket* 44827.
6. *See* unpublished response of the British National Consumer Council to the CAA Consultation Paper, March 1987, Annex 2, p. 3, no. 11.
7. Ibid., p. 4, no. 14; *The Avmark Aviation Economist*, June 1987, p. 15.
8. Unpublished response of the British National Consumer Council to the CAA Consultation Paper, March 1987, Annex 2, p. 5, no. 18.
9. Renton/Gaudin, Reserving Judgement, p. 19.

the passenger by allowing him to make his travel planning or arrangements himself without the assistance of a possibly biased travel agent: the availability of CRS services on home computer networks and the installation of CRSs on corporate premises. But given the bias of the systems which will hardly cease to exist as long as the airlines are CRS vendors, this development puts the passenger at the risk of suffering from the bias without even the theoretical opportunity to be helped around the bias by a professional. Already these professionals with all their expertise and experience may fall a victim to the sophistication of CRSs – an occasional private user will ordinarily be even less aware of the traps and about his possibilities to avoid them.

C. CONCLUSION

The identification of the passenger's benefits and disadvantages caused by the use and developments of CRSs showed that the passenger's position is heavily influenced by the fairness of the competition. If competition between airline CRS-vendors and have-nots or between larger and smaller CRS-vendors suffers, so will the passenger. With growing marketing power of a few and resulting market dominance of those few, the passenger's choice gets more and more limited.

Competition is the key factor when it comes to optimizing the passenger's position. Size as such and concentration is not necessarily bad: it can reduce redundancies, lower costs and increase productivity with a possibility of a resulting benefit for the passenger. But this benefit will not be achieved if there is no or not enough competition so that the large companies have no inducement to pass ower costs on to the passengers. CRSs may have the result of reducing competition as only few have the financial strength to develop them and everybody depends on them. Norman Minetta, Chairman of the U.S. House of Representatives Aviation Subcommittee, thinks that the CRS structure has contributed to the 'rush of airline mergers' because many airlines without CRSs believe they must merge in order to compete effectively against CRS vendor airlines.[10]

The creation of an industry wide, neutral CRS seems not to be a viable alternative, as carriers appear not to be willing to get together for the creation of such a system if there are too many companies involved. The NIBS activities[11] did not come to fruition and neither did the AEA project

---

10. *Travel Management Daily*, September 29, 1986.
11. *See supra*, Chapter III, A VI, p. 35; *see also infra*, Chapter V, C I, pp. 61-62.

GDS. [12] Maybe the smaller joint ventures (Amadeus and Galileo)[13] will be more successful. The systems created by these groups will possibly be more 'neutral' than CRSs owned by one carrier or a smaller number. However, the risk remains that these new systems will be designed in a way that gives the owners a competitive edge over the non-owners. And in any event, it has not been shown yet that 'unbiased systems' actually are feasible. Due to the limited space on one screen there will always be some algorithms that determine the order of display – and the carrier whose services appear at the end of the display will be able to give reasons why the algorithms are unjust, biased. According to Bruce Cunningham, Project Director of NIBS, the NIBS Interest Group never came to a final conclusion what a neutral display of air services should look like.[14] This means that the promulgation of hard and fast rules by governments is unlikely to result in CRSs that will satisfy everybody.

But competition in itself is not sufficient in order to increase the passenger's benefits derived from CRSs. The passenger also has to become aware of what is at stake for him when CRSs are used. If a passenger does not know that the results of a travel agent's searches in a CRS will most likely differ substantially depending on the system they use, then the passenger will see no need to question the result of that search, and he will not consider to start shopping if he thinks the agent is doing this for him. It appears that the passengers still view the travel agent as a neutral intermediary between vendors of services and his clients. This function, however, is threatened: the bias of CRSs as well as developments that compromise the agent's neutrality[15] have started to change the traditional role of the travel agent. It will be important to alert the passengers and to establish a comprehension on their side of the changing roles of those involved in the distribution of air services.

This will have to be borne in mind when analyzing in the next chapter the policy options available to those who actively participate in this field.

---

12. *See supra*, Chapter III, B II, p. 41.
13. *See supra*, Chapter III, B II, p. 41-43.
14. Statement made in an interview with the author in Montréal, May 26, 1987.
15. *See supra*, Chapter III, A VI, pp. 35-37.

CHAPTER V

POLICY OPTIONS

A. NATIONAL APPROACHES

National rulemaking in order to solve CRS related problems has one general drawback: the operation of CRSs is, just as aviation itself, not limited to one state. The adoption of separate legal regimes of different scope, specificity and severity could therefore create 'CRS-heavens' and interfere with equal opportunity to compete on an international basis.[1] Beyond this general argument, there are also specific reasons why national approaches are not very promising.

I. THE 1984 CAB CRS RULES

The basis for the CAB's rulemaking[2] were three conclusions: the CAB held that the marketpower of CRS owners, the character of CRSs as essential facilities, and the consumer injury and deception found in the way CRSs were operated warranted the adoption of its rules.

Certainly the CAB rules have put an end to a number of those practices that gave rise to complaints about CRSs. But already a few months after the adoption of the CAB rules, it became necessary to request the CRS vendors to eliminate 'secondary displays' which the CRS vendors had introduced because the CAB CRS-rules only prohibited bias in 'primary' displays.[3]

Two years later, the U.S. Department of Transportation (DOT) had to react to continuing complaints concerning excessive booking fees, liquidated damages clauses in the vendor-agent agreements and the amount of incremental revenues generated by CRSs.

---

1. Cf. Raben, CRS, p. 25.
2. Cf. *supra*, Chapter III, A I a, pp. 24-25.
3. *See supra*, Chapter III, A IV, pp. 29-30.

On February 2, 1987, the DOT issued an order requiring CRS vendors to submit special reports in order to update the Department's knowledge about the status of CRS competition and about the effects of certain CRS practices. This order had become necessary because despite the promulgation of the CRS rules questions had been raised about the potential of CRS vendors to exert market power and thereby influence competition in the airline industry.[4] The information which the CRS vendors are required to supply is very extensive and costly to compile. The CRS vendors had to have written computer programs for the sole purpose of providing the DOT with the required information.[5] The CRS vendors did not contest the order (unlike the original 1984 CRS rules). This complaisance becomes understandable if one considers how difficult it will be for the DOT to come to a clear conclusion for instance with respect to the question if booking fees the vendors charge other carriers are excessive.

Another move of the DOT may be more promising: the DOT has given Notice of a Proposed Rulemaking[6] in order to resolve problems with on-time schedule performance of air services. Unrealistic schedule times allowed carriers to obtain more favourable screen displays in CRSs and has therefore become a widespread practice.[7]

But even if more problems caused by the operation can be solved, it remains very doubtful if this way of 'patchwork'-regulation should be continued. The regulations will have to become more and more specific without effectively excluding more sophisticated abuses of CRSs by ingenious vendors. Regulations like the CAB's 1984 CRS rules necessarily are only a reaction which means that CRS vendors are not restricted in employing their practices until the rules have become effective. And the legislative process so far has been time consuming and costly because of the hearings, reports and investigations – the results hardly justify the effort.

II. DIVESTITURE

The harshest measure available to a government in order to solve problems caused by unfair practices in the operation of CRSs would be divestiture.[8]

4. See *supra*, Chapter III, A V, pp. 32-34, and U.S. Department of Transportation, Information Directives Concerning Computer Reservations Systems, issued 2-2-1987, *Docket* 44643, p. 1.
5. According to Henry J. Feinberg, General Manager – Pacific for Covia, who was interviewed by the author in Chicago, July 14, 1987.
6. *Docket* 44827.
7. See *also supra*, Chapter III, A IV, pp. 31-32.
8. For an analysis of CRS antitrust implications under U.S. law *see* Saunders, The Antitrust Implications.

Divestiture, i.e. separation of CRS ownership from the airline parent, might facilitate entry of new CRSs and increase CRS competition, because the entry advantage of a dominant carrier in a given market would be eliminated: nowadays a travel agent tends to opt for a CRS which is provided by the most important carrier in the region where the agent is located; if CRSs would not be marketed any more by carriers entry could become easier for competitors. Also, if bookings fees charged by the vendors should indeed be supra-competitive now, this market distortion would be eliminated if non-airlines would be CRS vendors as all carriers would have to pay booking fees to the vendor.[9] And there is also the expectation that divestiture would reduce bias in CRSs as a non-airline CRS owner cannot earn incremental revenues from the operation of a CRS and is therefore more inclined to unbias his system.

The market power of CRSs would remain, though, with the risk that while all carriers are treated equally booking fees might still be excessive.[10]

While there have been advocates of divestiture there is little support for it today. U.S. Senator Nancy Kassebaum in 1985 considered divestiture a possibility but said that the government 'must be careful not to simply shift the possibility for abuse to an entity outside the airline industry.'[11] The U.S. Department of Justice (DOJ) in its 1985 report on CRSs concluded that the costs of the various divestiture alternatives are very high, and the possibility of service disruption is great. The DOJ held non-airline vendors may not have the same incentive to upgrade a system and to keep it on the frontier of technology. It further expressed its concern that economies of scope between operating an airline and operating a CRS could be lost by requiring divestiture and that certain skills and capabilities possessed by carriers and contributing to the success of CRSs could not be transferred with divestiture. DOJ also pointed out that without a possibility to limit the ability of an independent CRS to 'sell bias' to the carriers, the situation after divestiture would be indistinguishable from the pre-rules era.[12] The DOJ report therefore did not recommend divestiture.

Divestiture also would supply the CRS owners which would be required to divest with very large amounts of money. This would place them in such an advantageous financial position that there is some reason to be concerned about the competitive effect of such a monetary armament.[13]

9. Department of Justice, *1985 Report*, pp. 64-65.
10. Ibid.
11. *Aviation Daily*, March 22, 1985.
12. Department of Justice, *1985 Report*, pp. 66 et seq.
13. This concern was voiced by Cindy Burbank of the U.S. DOT Office of Policy and International Affairs, in an interview with the author in Washington, D.C. on July 15, 1987.

When adopting its CRS-rules the CAB in the Supplementary Information gave several reasons which made it determine that divestiture was not appropriate.[14] Two of them still hold: divestiture would take years and certain efficiencies can only be attained by vertical integration into the CRS industry by air carriers (economies of scope). The conclusion that the objectives pursued by the CAB can be accomplished by adopting general rules has proven incorrect.

However, considering the pro's and con's of divestiture, it cannot be assumed with a satisfying degree of certainty that divestiture would actually lead to substantial improvements. For the passenger divestiture could mean increased costs because of lost economies of scope, reduced pace of development of systems, and risks of maintained bias because of relations between new CRS owners and carriers ('sold bias').

B. INTERNATIONAL APPROACHES

Numerous international organizations, on the governmental level as well as from the private sector have shown some interest in the CRS industry. Some bodies are currently involved in studies and they will take a stand only after the completion of these studies and after discussing the results. However, it is not too early to make some comments on the opportunities for these organizations to pay regard to the passengers' interests in their deliberations.

I. ICAO

In March 1986, the ICAO Council approved a recommendation adopted in October 1985 by the Third Air Transport Conference and directed that a study concerning CRSs be carried out with the assistance of the ICAO Panel of Experts on the Machinery for the Establishment of International Fares and Rates (Fares and Rates Panel or Panel).

The Third Air Transport Conference had also recommended that the ICAO Council formulate recommendations whose purpose would be to avoid abuse of CRSs at the international level, in order to enhance fair competition between airlines and to protect the travelling public.[15]

---

14. U.S. Civil Aeronautics Board, *Regulation ER-1385*, Economic Regulations, Issuance of Part 255, *Docket* 41686, p. 51.
15. *ICAO Doc.* FRP/9-WP/2, 21/10/86 (Working Paper for the ninth meeting of the Fares and Rates Panel), p. 1; *see also ICAO Doc.* FRP/9 (Report of the ninth meeting of the Fares and Rates Panel), p. 15.

The Panel during its ninth meeting reviewed and amended a list of examples of CRS bias and a list of examples of other types of market manipulation by CRS vendors.[16] The Panel felt that these examples should be examined in greater detail with a view to understanding more fully their impact and to determining whether and how they should be addressed by governments.

A questionnaire which had been prepared by the ICAO Secretariat and which was reviewed by the Panel was sent in March 1987 to states in order to solicit information with respect to states' policies and practices regarding or affecting the regulation of CRSs and in order to develop an inventory of CRSs and their scope of application. ICAO hopes to complete the main work on CRSs in 1988.[17]

According to a Working Paper presented by the Secretariat for the Panel's ninth meeting, one approach for ICAO might be to consider developing some general recommendations for multilateral application. Another, not necessarily exclusive, approach which might prove more effective in remedying CRS problems could be the development of a suitable clause for insertion in bilateral agreements as required, along with guidelines for the regulation of CRSs by individual states.[18]

While at this early stage it is entirely open what recommendations the ICAO Council will eventually adopt it can be said that ICAO's contribution to resolving CRS related issues could be extremely important. The study with its information input of – theoretically – 156 member states will be a very valuable basis for the determination of the global CRS situation and of governmental policies and practices regarding these systems. A multilateral instrument on the issue is not very likely to deal successfully with the problems: it would take too long to develop it, and the various states' positions probably are too different in order to allow a meaningful agreement. Also very specific recommendations with respect to national regulation of CRS activities can hardly be expected to lead to rules which are better suited to put an end to abuse of CRSs that the CAB 1984 CRS rules which have resulted in more sophisticated ways of abuse rather than abolishing it.

Guidance material or model clauses for inclusion in bilateral air transport agreements might be the key to success. Because of the great importance of CRSs as marketing tools bilateral air transport agreements certainly are an apt place for provisions regarding CRSs. And bilaterals can be specific enough in order to address effectively problems encountered between the

16. *See infra*, Annex C, pp. 89-93.
17. According to C.B. Lyle, ICAO Air Transport Bureau, in a presentation given to the 9th UFTAA Automation Seminar, held in Nice, 15 April 1987.
18. *ICAO Doc.* FRP/9-WP/2, 21/10/86, p. 9.

agreeing states. One could even argue that bilaterals that provide for 'equal and fair opportunity to compete' already cover CRS operations.[19] If bilateral air transport agreements will contribute to more competition on an international basis, the end of unfair practices with respect to CRSs could be near. New entrants in the CRS market may be unlikely – but competition could be achieved by facilitating competition from already existent CRSs by giving them equal access to countries where their owners want to offer their services. And competition appears to be the decisive factor when attempting to reduce market dominance and resulting unfair practices. Passengers would be enabled to shop for air services in various CRSs and the dependance of agents and 'have-not' carriers could be reduced.

It would be in the best interest of everybody affected by the operation of CRSs if the participation of its member states in the CRS study would enable the ICAO Council to finish its study soon and to formulate recommendations which, according to the Third Air Transport Conference's recommendation, are meant 'to enhance competition between airlines and to protect the travelling public.'

II. ECAC

The European Civil Aviation Conference (ECAC), which is comprised of 22 European states, also has become active on CRS issues.

ECAC has expressed its view that ECAC airlines are discriminated against by the way U.S. CRSs are operated and that this prevents fair and equal opportunity for ECAC carriers to compete.[20]

ECAC in its presentation for the Tenth ECAC/U.S. Meeting on North Atlantic Pricing (October, 1986) further emphasized the need to protect the consumer interest. ECAC predicted that unless the problems it had identified[21] were resolved within a reasonable time, there would be implications which would need to be reviewd by ECAC Member States both in the context of the Memorandum of Understanding and more widely.

While ECAC expressed its trust that the problems could be resolved between ECAC and the United States on a multilateral basis,[22] this has

19. Cf. Fahy, Regulation, p. 240.
20. Unpublished presentation by the ECAC delegations for the Tenth ECAC/U.S. Meeting on North Atlantic Pricing, Washington, 14-17 October 1986, Document NAP/10-WP/2, 14/10/86, agenda item 2b)iv): Fair and equal competitive opportunities.
21. Through flight numbers for flights involving change of aircraft, preference for on-line connections over inter-line connections, code-sharing, dual display, possibility to input unduly favourable flying times, ibid., pp. 2-3.
22. Ibid., p. 1.

become doubtful recently. U.S. and European systems were demonstrated and discussed in detail in Washington, D.C. and in Paris, but it appears as if the U.S. were less determined to deal with these problems on a multilateral basis.[23] One reason for this reluctance may be the fact that the current DOT investigation[24] is still underway. ECAC even contributed to this investigation with a submission in April 1987.[25]

ECAC also has started to collect factual information regarding CRSs in intra-European air transport. ECAC aspires to produce guidelines to ensure free access to CRSs and to achieve display of flights in a non-discriminatory way.[26]

The latter approach resembles ICAO's activities and it could become an important one if it will not take too much time to find formulae which can be agreed upon by ECAC member states. The necessity for intra-European improvements are evidenced by the action of the EEC Commission when Sabena wanted to exclude London European Airways from Saphir display.[27] Very much is at stake for smaller carriers in Europe – and for the passenger as in many instances these small carriers are willing to offer very competitive services in order to establish themselves. However, without fair access to European CRSs their chances are heavily impaired.

III. EUROPEAN ECONOMIC COMMUNITY (EEC)

An act by the EEC in the CRS field that has gained some prominence was the intervention by the European Commission in the London European Airways – Sabena case.[28] This intervention was successful as Sabena on May 25, 1987 informed the Commission that it was prepared to grant London European Airways access to Sabena's CRS Saphir. If this action really means that the battle for access to CRSs is already won in the EEC[29] remains to be seen; however, the speed of the Commission's action[30] shows

23. A similar stand was taken by the U.S. Member of the ICAO Fares and Rates Panel at the Ninth Meeting, November 24 to December 5 1986, Report of the Meeting, ICAO Doc. FRP/9, p. 16.
24. *See supra*, Chapter III, A V, pp. 32-34.
25. Enclosure to letter EC 9/8.4/20.2 EC 9/8.4/21-288; in this document ECAC also highlighted the practice of 'screen padding', i.e. the display of additional information resulting in less favourable display positions for subsequent flights.
26. *The Avmark Aviation Economist*, June 1987, p. 15.
27. *See supra* Chapter IV, B, p. 49.
28. *See supra* Chapter IV, B, p. 49.
29. *The Avmark Aviation Economist*, June 1987, p. 15.
30. London European Airways lodged its complaint with the Commission on April 22, 1987; the Commission on April 28, 1987 ordered an investigation; on April 30, 1987,

its determination to deal with CRS discrimination[31] if it amounts to a breach of Article 86 of the Treaty of Rome.

On the other hand, the Commission had drafted a Regulation which would grant certain exemptions from Article 85 of the Treaty of Rome. This Regulation would entitle the Commission, among others, to declare that Article 85(1) of the Treaty would not apply

'in respect of agreements, decisions or concerted practices which have as their object . . . the following:

. . .

common purchase, development and operation of computer reservation systems relating to timetabling, reservations and ticketing by air transport undertakings, on condition that air carriers of Member States have access to such systems on equal terms, that participating carriers have their services listed on a non-discriminatory basis, and also that any participant may withdraw from the system on giving reasonable notice;

. . .'

This and the other exemptions provided for by the draft regulation were meant to win the support of those EEC member states that were reluctant to accept an EEC package to reform European aviation and to liberalize it. This package in June 1987 failed to achieve the unanimous approval of all EEC member states because Spain and the United Kingdom could not settle their differences on the implications for Gibraltar.

The many exemptions provided for by the draft regulation certainly would have compromised the liberalisation effect of the package, but at least there was the expectation of some benefits for the air traveller. With respect to the CRS-exemption, though, it appears that the EC Commission should not only be concerned about access on equal terms for member state carriers. It is in the best interest of the air traveller if competition is

---

→ the Commission's Competition Officials accompanied by a representative of the Belgian Ministry of Economic Affairs carried out an investigation at the offices of Sabena (once described as a 'dawn raid', *see The Avmark Aviation Economist*, June 1987, p. 15) and on May 7, 1987, the Directorate-General of Competition notified Sabena of its intention to adopt interim measures obliging Sabena to accept London European Airways in Saphir; press-release of the Spokeman's Service of the Commission of the European Communities, June 3, 1987, 1P (87) 215.

31. *See The Avmark Aviation Economist*, June 1987, p. 15; but cf. Raben, CRS, p. 25 who in 1986 considered the EC Commission to be insufficiently aware of the significance of CRS problems.

supported on a global basis, i.e. also non-member state carriers should have equal access to any CRSs. If there is a need to ensure that European carriers are treated equally in non-EEC CRSs, a reciprocity requirement would be a possibility.[32]

The exemption for CRSs as such might be viewed as anti-competitive, too. But the draft regulation included in Article 7, subsection 2 would have allowed the Commission to withdraw the benefit of the block exemption and to take all appropriate measures if it found that an agreement, decision or concerted practice had effects that are incompatible with Article 85(3) or are prohibited by Article 86 of the Treaty of Rome; this would have been a safequard against abuses. Also a certain degree of European cooperation appears to be necessary for the preservation of competition: American CRSs are so much bigger than European systems that the latter might not be able to survive U.S. CRS entry into Europe unless they would be allowed to form joint ventures.

But in the light of the failure of the liberalisation package of the EEC, it appears that any CRS alignments could become subjected to stricter scrutiny in the future. In any event the EC Commission appears to be willing to use its tools to prevent abuses; if the results will be similarly successful as in the London European Airways/Sabena case, the passenger has reason to expect substantial support from Brussels as the competition rules of the EEC provide protection against many anti-competitive practices.[33]

C. NON-GOVERNMENTAL APPROACHES

I. IATA

Also IATA has been actively involved with the developments in the CRS industry.[34] In September 1984, its Traffic Committee established a working

32. Section 255.9 (b) of the CAB 1984 CRS rules (see infra: Annex B Part I) exempts a system vendor from compliance with the rules with respect to a foreign carrier if that carrier or its affiliate operates a CRS that does not display U.S. carriers' flights equally.
33. Paper presented by the International Organization of Consumer Unions (IOCU) to the European Civil Aviation Conference, Eurpol 24-3/6th 1987, agenda item 2 (preliminary discussion on market access, including exchange of views on CRS), p. 7.
34. This information is based on several interviews which the author had with IATA officials in Geneva and Montréal: A.D. Groenewege, Director Industry Affairs, Dr. Ludwig Weber, Counsel, J. Wineberg, Coordinator Industry Automation Telecommunications, all Geneva, June 16, 1987; Milford L. Coor, Senior Counsel, Michael Feldman, →

group 'to determine whether a neutral computerized reservation system (CRS) is a viable proposal'. This proposal was called Neutral Industry Booking System (NIBS) and eventually was abandoned.[35] However, as it was pointed out in a presentation by IATA to ECAC in April 1987, a number of basic principles which should be observed in any industry proposal for a neutral CRS were established in the course of the NIBS discussions.[36] These principles may have some bearing on the CRS products of the two European groups which are currently in formation.

Because IATA is also committed to supporting fair competition among its members, it has studied the question of how best to ensure that no single party is ever able to gain a monopoly control over any of the elements of information that drive CRSs. Work is being done known as AIMS (Airline Information Management System) with the objective to facilitate the operation of existing CRSs and to encourage the establishment of new systems. And a proposal is being prepared to establish an industry international fares database that would guarantee access to complete fares information to all CRS operators and other parties. Similar work is going on with respect to the distribution of schedules and availability data. Also the question of developing new technology that would make the development of new CRSs easier and cheaper is being adressed by IATA with a view to prevent unhealthy dominance by any single party in this field.

IATA has realized that 'bias as such always has been and most likely will remain to be found in air transport information. While wilfully distortive forms of bias have substantially been eliminated in the U.S., more subtle forms remain. IATA also has expressed doubts that governments are able to react quickly enough in order to prevent abuses effectively by regulation. IATA also is concerned about the bureaucratic costs of such regulation which would have to be borne ultimately by the customer whom the regulations are designed to protect. IATA therefore advocates policies which encourage many CRS entrants into the field rather than regulations which attempt to proscribe the behaviour of a few. IATA's view that a healthy competition among CRS vendors is the best protection was also supported by the International Chamber of Commerce in a policy state-

---

Consultant Industry Automation, Louis Haeck, Assistant Corporate Secretary, all Montréal in May/June 1987.
35. *See supra* Chapter III, A VI, p. 35.
36. Unpublished presentation by Eddie Spry (IATA) to ECAC on CRSs in Paris, April 8, 1987.

ment on CRSs which recommended a reliance on market forces, tempered by a framework of government rules.[37]

It is not very likely that IATA's hopes for many new CRS entrants will materialize. The costs for a new system are too high. However, if IATA's work will not do more than contribute to the facilitation of existing systems and, therefore, hopefully to the reduction in costs, it would be worthwhile. But if one realistically considers IATA's position, one has to admit that IATA's activities have to stop where they would affect IATA's members' competitive opportunities. Short of that, the passenger could benefit from IATA's continuing involvement.

II. INTERNATIONAL FOUNDATION OF AIRLINE PASSENGERS' ASSOCIATIONS (IFAPA)

IFAPA is a non-profit making organization established in Switzerland with the purpose to promote, to research and to represent the interests of airline passengers with governments, airlines and the travel trade at international, regional and national levels.

IFAPA is concerned that too much of the CRS discussion has focused on airline considerations and a higher priority needs to be given to the passengers' interests.[38] IFAPA therefore included in its 1987 survey of passenger preferences also questions on CRSs. The initial results of this survey indicate that a large number of passengers does not realize that their bookings are made through CRSs. A small pilot survey in the United Kingdom also showed that a significant number of travellers was not aware of the role of CRSs.[39]

IFAPA consequently emphasizes the need to inform the travelling public about the key criteria on which CRS displays are based so that passengers can objectively examine their options.[40] In IFAPA's view each CRS, including those available on home computers, should contain information about the vendors of a system, preferential flight display, the order in which flights are listed. This information should be passed on to customers who request

---

37. Policy Statement adopted by the Executive Board (50th Session, 11 June 1987) of the International Chamber of Commerce, Policy & Programme Department, *Document* No. 310/346 Rev. 3.
38. *Aviation Daily*, June 23, 1986, p. 470.
39. Plane Facts, *News from IFAPA*, Issue 6, June 1987.
40. Plane Facts, *News from IFAPA*, Issue 4, December 1986/January 1987, p. 1.

it. IFAPA further holds that passengers should be educated to understand problems of bias and the need to request the key criteria.[41]

Particularly the latter point is of critical importance. It will not improve the passenger's situation if several CRS options are available, i.e. if there is real CRS competition in a given market, unless the passenger is aware of the implications of the use of a certain system. If the passenger understands that a travel agent is not necessarily determined to work in his best interest as a neutral consultant but may work according to his own lines of policy and that he will use a CRS that is designed to work as a marketing tool primarily for the vendor of the system, then the passenger might take full advantage of the systems by making their capabilities work to his benefit or by shopping around in different systems. This means that competition and an enhanced public awareness of CRSs and their basic features have to complement one another in order to achieve optimal results for the traveller.

Considering this one has to keep in mind that Section 255.4 (b) (2) and (c) (3) of the CAB 1984 CRS rules[42] already require system vendors to provide any person, i.e. passengers, too, upon request the criteria used in ordering flights, the weight given to each criterion, and information on connecting points and criteria used for the display of connecting flights.

This provision would probably have a greater practical impact if this information would not only be available upon request from the system vendor, but from a travel agent as well, i.e. by directly storing the information in the CRS. But the availability of the information is only of secondary importance. Primarily it should be viewed as the task of governments as well as of consumer organizations to alert travellers to the great effect the use of a certain CRS has on their travel arrangements. If this awareness can be established the passenger will automatically start to take the proper actions.

41. Letter from Geoffrey Lipman, Executive Director, IFAPA, published in the *International Herald Tribune*, January 23, 1987.
42. *See infra* Annex B, Part III.

CHAPTER VI

PROTECTION OF PRIVACY AND TRANSBORDER DATA FLOW

The operation of CRSs is subject to legislation on a national level as well as it is affected by international instruments. This is particularly true where the transfer of information stored in a CRS from one country to another (transborder data flow = TDF) becomes necessary.

TDF in a CRS may be accomplished in a multi-access system as well as through a single-access system. In a multi-access system a communication switch enables a user to have access to systems of different participants. But also in a single-access system where a user has access only to the vendor's system he will generally have the opportunity to make reservations on other carriers' flights.[1] If in these cases the carrier on whose flight a reservation is made resides in another country than the user (or the CRS-vendor) a transborder data flow takes place. Often SITA (Société Internationale de Télécommunications Aéronautiques) or its U.S. equivalent ARINC (Aeronautical Radio Incorporated) will actually handle the transfer of information.[2] However, some airlines operate their own telecommunications systems by renting telecommunications lines.

Individual as well as national interests may be affected by TDF. The information stored in CRSs is personal information which the respective individuals may not wish to be used for other purposes than those connected with their trip.

The protection of infant industries, informational sovereignty,[3] the protection of intellectual property rights, and the national security are concerns which induce countries to consider or to promulgate regulations that restrict TDF. This is the case even for those countries which are in

---

1. Under the agreements between those other carriers and the vendor.
2. SITA as well as ARINC provide telecommunication facilities for airlines.
3. *See* OECD, An Exploration of Legal Issues in Information and Communication Technologies, pp. 34 et seq.

general committed to a policy which furthers TDF.[4] States may feel tempted, too, to use TDF as a source of income by taxing it.[5]

These interests have resulted in extensive national data-protection/privacy-protection legislation.[6] The OECD and the Council of Europe have adopted instruments which are aimed at harmonizing data-protection standards on an international basis. A private institution, the Atwater Institute has launched an ambitious project with the objective to act as a catalyst in the creation of an international policy framework governing TDF. And many organizations, national as well as international ones, both from the private and the public (governmental, intergovernmental) sectors tackle the problem.

In general, CRS vendors so far have experienced little or no problems in the area of transborder data flow. Covia, however, United Airlines' affiliate did encounter difficulties in this respect when it attempted to market its CRS in South Korea. This question then was raised as an issue in the course of U.S./South Korea bilateral air transport negotiations.[7]

A. THE OECD GUIDELINES

On September 23, 1980 the OECD Council adopted a 'Recommendation Concerning Guidelines Governing the Protection of Privacy and Transborder Flows of Personal Data'.[8] These Guidelines have no binding force on the OECD member countries. It is merely recommended that member countries take the principles contained in the Guidelines into account in their domestic legislation. However, all member countries have indicated that they intend to adhere to the Guidelines,[9] with the exception of Ireland (which is nonetheless not opposed to the Guidelines). The purpose of the Guidelines is not only the protection of privacy. As stated in the Preamble the Council is determined 'to advance the free flow of information between member countries and to avoid the creation of unjustified obstacles to the development of economic and social relations among Member countries.'

---

4. A comprehensive analysis of the interest constellation can be found in: Sauvant, International Transactions in Services, pp. 154 et seq.
5. Cf. OECD, An Exploration of Legal Issues in Information and Communication Technologies, pp. 105/106.
6. Sauvant, p. 156 gives a list of these national laws.
7. Information obtained from Henry J. Feinberg, General Manager – Pacific of Covia, in an interview which took place in Chicago on July 14, 1987.
8. OECD, Guidelines on the Protection of Privacy and Transborder Data Flows of Personal Data (Paris: OECD, 1981).
9. Sauvant, International Transactions in Services, p. 158.

In accordance with this determination the Council recommends that member countries endeavour to remove or avoid creating obstacles to transborder flows of personal data. As Guideline (2) sets forth, the Guidelines apply to personal data, i.e. information relating to an identified or identifiable individual (definition of 'personal data' in Guideline (1)(b)). However, there is a restriction in Guideline (2): the application of the Guidelines is limited to those personal data, whether in the public or private sector, 'which because of the manner in which they are processed, or because of their nature or the context in which they are used, pose a danger to privacy and individual liberties.' While the true meaning of this limitation is certainly open to some argument, it can hardly be challenged that information stored in a CRS poses a danger to privacy. If such information becomes accessible it will allow to determine which trips the 'data subject' made, when he travelled, how much money he spent on the tickets, possibly personal preferences connected with travel, where he picked up a rental car, in which hotel he stayed, which theatre tickets he bought, etc. Objections to public disclosure of this information appears to be warranted. These data can hardly be called data 'which obviously do not contain any risk to privacy and individual liberties'. Were the data of this nature, an exclusion from the application of the Guidelines could be considered under Guideline (3)(b).[10]

The principles concerning TDF are set out in Part Three of the Guidelines:

'15. Member countries should take into consideration the implications for other Member countries of domestic processing and re-export of personal data.

16. Member countries should take all reasonable and appropriate steps to ensure that transborder flows of personal data, including transit through a Member country, are uninterrupted and secure.

17. A Member country should refrain from restricting transborder flows of personal data between itself and another Member country except where the latter does not yet substantially observe these Guidelines or where the re-export of such data would circumvent its domestic privacy legislation. A Member country may also impose restrictions in respect of certain categories of personal data for which its domestic privacy legislation includes specific regulations in view of the nature of those data and

---

10. '3. These Guidelines should not be interpreted as preventing:

. . .

(b) The exclusion from the application of the Guidelines of personal data which obviously do not contain any risk to privacy and individual liberties. Or

. . . .'.

for which the other Member country provides no equivalent protection.

    18. Member countries should avoid developing laws, policies and practices in the name of the protection of privacy and individual liberties, which would create obstacles to transborder flows of personal data that would exceed requirements for such protection.'

Despite their non-binding nature, the OECD Guidelines are of some significance as they tackle the TDF issue on an international basis.[11] This could contribute to the resolution of the problem created by uncoordinated and conflicting national laws and regulations. Nonetheless, IATA has concluded that a flexible legislation that would take into account the imperatives of international airline telematics would be better than the OECD Guidelines. This conclusion is based on the assessment that the constraints supposed to protect the right to privacy will hamper the international airlines' day-to-day operations and may ultimately have an adverse effect on the quality of the services offered by the airline to the customer.[12] IATA also emphasizes the costs data-protection needs can cause.[13]

    It appears questionable if this is really a valid point. The passenger will not be opposed to the transfer of information to another country as long as it serves his interest, i.e. to facilitate his flight. It does not serve his interest, though, if the collected data are used for other purposes, e.g. for marketing other products of the CRS vendor or for making profit by selling the data. The protection of privacy is a concern of the passenger no less in air transport than in other industries. And it is not so much experience of misuse but its possibility which justifies protection of privacy legislation.

B. CONVENTION OF THE COUNCIL OF EUROPE FOR THE PROTECTION OF INDIVIDUALS WITH REGARD TO AUTOMATED PROCESSING OF PERSONAL DATA

The Convention of the Council of Europe for the Protection of Individuals with Regard to Automated Processing of Personal Data (Council of Europe Convention)[14] was opened for signature on 28 January 1981 and entered

11. In this context it must be kept in mind, though, that the OECD has only a limited number of member countries from a fairly homogeneous group.
12. Haeck, Les Flux de Données Transfrontières. Cf. Eser, Impact of Automation, p. 11.
13. Author unknown, Airline Data Exchange Endangered? – here an IATA officer is quoted who gives an example for the potential cost consequences of even small changes: he estimates that the adoption of even small changes: he estimates that the adoption of three-letter airline designators instead of the currently used two-letter designators may cause costs in excess of $200 million only for changing the industry's software.
14. European Treaty Series, No. 108 (Strasbourg: Council of Europe, 1981), pp. 2-11.

into force on 1 October 1985. It is open for accession also to states not members of the Council of Europe (Art. 23). Unlike the OECD Guidelines the Council of Europe Convention is a binding international treaty.

The Convention is intended to protect the privacy of individuals, whatever their nationality or residence with regard to automatic processing of personal data relating to them (Art. 1). In chapter II basic principles for data protection are spelled out which the contracting parties are to give effect to in their domestic laws (Art. 4). Chapter III deals in its sole article with TDF:

'CHAPTER III – TRANSBORDER DATA FLOWS

Article 12
Transborder flows of personal data
and domestic law

1. The following provisions shall apply to the transfer across national borders, by whatever medium, of personal data undergoing automatic processing or collected with a view to their being automatically processed.

2. A Party shall not, for the sole purpose of the protection of privacy, prohibit or subject to special authorisation transborder flows of personal data going to the territory of another Party.

3. Nevertheless, each party shall be entitled to derogate from the provisions of paragraph 2:

a. insofar as its legislation includes specific regulations for certain categories of personal data or of automated personal data files, because of the nature of those data or those files, except where the regulations of the other Party provide an equivalent protection;

b. when the transfer is made from its territory to the territory of a non-Contracting State through the intermediary of the territory of another Party, in order to avoid such transfers resulting in circumvention of the legislation of the Party referred to at the beginning of this paragraph.'

C. GENERAL AGREEMENT ON INFORMATION TRANSFER/TRADE (GAIT)

An innovative and ambitious project is under way under the auspices of the Atwater Institute (The World Information Economy Centre), located in Montréal).

I. ATWATER INSTITUTE

The Atwater Institute commenced its operations on July 1, 1985. Its goal is to preserve and enhance international trade and exchange in information and information-intensive services and manufacture. The activities of the Institute are financed by 'Standard Chartered Member Commitments' of Can.$50.000 over 3 years per member. Currently there are 12 members from the private sector in Canada, U.S.A., U.K., and Bermuda. They are companies and one private individual which share a particular interest in the field of information and communication with a focus on public policy issues. The Director General of the Atwater Institute is the Swedish diplomat Knut O.H.A, Hammarskjöld, Director General of IATA until 1984.[15]

II. PRINCIPAL PROJECT: GAIT

The principal project of the Atwater Institute is 'to act as a catalyst in the creation of an international policy framework for a core sector of the world economy, leading to a General Agreement on Information Transfer/Trade (GAIT).'[16] In furtherance of this project the Atwater Institute commissioned an analysis of the prospects and difficulties inherent in an Atwater proposal for an international policy framework for trade in and transfer of information and information-based services.[17]

This framework shall strike a balance between the needs and ambitions of users and providers of information services the world over while at the same time meeting legitimate national and individual needs and aspirations.[18] This framework is meant to preserve maximum freedom and flexibility for the users of information (both institutional and individual) and to be acceptable to the developing as well as the developed countries.[19] The objective is to avoid the spreading of the regulation over numerous international organizations and institutions or the resolution of the prob-

15. *Source* Atwater Institute; Aims, Projects and People.
16. Ibid.
17. This analysis was published: Grey, The Elements of a General Agreement on Information Transfer/Trade (GAIT), 1986.
18. Atwater Institute, *Newsletter*, January 1987, p. 2.
19. Ibid.; *see also* Abridged Version of a speech given by the Director General of the Atwater Institute, Knut Hammarskjöld, during the Atwater 1986 Conference, in: Atwater Institute, Newsletter February 1987. Cf. Hammarskjöld, Conceptual Evolution Caused – and Necessitated – by Technological Advancement: Transition to Information-Based-Society – A Case in Point.

lem on an individual national level. During a conference held in Montréal in November 1986 concern was expressed relating to the spread of data protection laws with provisions that varied from country to country as well as to the fragmentation of international activity on the information economy.[20]

This Conference together with various studies and a publication[21] formed the 'exploration phase' of the project. In a 'construction phase' and subsequently a 'consolidation phase' representative views from various sources shall be sought and a model framework shall be drafted, 'fine-tuned', and eventually presented to governmental and intergovernmental organizations for consideration and negotiations. The last phase is scheduled to be concluded by the end of 1989. More conferences, publications and studies will form parts of the phases to come.[22]

III. PROSPECTS FOR GAIT

Obviously at this early stage any predictions concerning a success or a failure of GAIT would be pure guesswork. So far only the 'exploration stage' of the project has been brought to an end. The 'model framework' has not been presented yet, let alone been discussed. However, the ultimate success of this uncommon approach to an issue which is of major concern to so many parties will depend on the appeal GAIT has to governments. Given the fact that the members of the Atwater Institute are entirely linked to the private sector some reluctance of governments to take over a project like GAIT can be anticipated. The interests of governments in transborder data flow and their positions also differ substantially, unlike with ICAO[23] for instance where the safety of air transport can be easily identified as a matter of common concern to all member states. This might further make some governments hesitate to consider a GAIT-proposal developed on the basis of the initiative of the Atwater Institute. It remains to be seen if the states will be able to agree on a meaningful framework for transborder data flow. If this framework will be based on a forthcoming Atwater proposal is even more questionable.

20. Atwater Institute, *Newsletter*, April 1987, p. 4.
21. Sauvant, International Transactions in Services: The Politics of Transborder Data Flows.
22. Atwater Institute, *Newsletter*, April 1987, p. 213.
23. ICAO in Hammarskjöld's view may serve as an inspiration for possible solutions, Atwater Institute, *Newsletter*, February 1987, p. 2.

D. OTHER TDF-FORA

TDF has been an issue in many different fora. In bilateral trade negotiations between the U.S. and other countries trade in service in general and issues related to TDF are discussed. The OECD continues to address TDF.[24] The Intergovernmental Bureau of Information (IBI) organizes conferences at which recommendations and resolutions concerning TDF are adopted.[25] IBI also established an International Consultative Commission on Transborder Data Flow Development. The Latin American Economic System (SELA) has been paying attention to trade in data services.[26] Also GATT has decided to launch negotiations on trade in services.[27] The United Nations Conference on Trade and Development (UNCTAD) has adopted a work program on services which can be expected to result in special attention being paid to TDF.[28] The International Telecommunication Union establishes the framework for the technical and operational aspects of TDF. It was even suggested that ITU consider the issues arising from the impact of telecommunications on – among others – the information flow.[29] The United Nations Commission and Centre on Transnational Corporations (UNCTC) have also dealt with TDF regularly.[30] The International Civil Aviation Organization (ICAO) has so far not become involved in the TDF discussion.[31]

E. CONCLUSION

Considering the developments outlined above the passenger's situation calls for two things: on the one hand a global framework on TDF which reduces unwarranted restrictions and does away with the highly complex mix of national and international regulations and avoids further fragmentation as this may indeed unnecessarily interfere with the use of CRSs which

---

24. On 11 April 1985 the OECD Council of Ministers adopted a Declaration on Transborder Data Flows, for the text and a discussion see Sauvant, pp. 237 et seq.
25. Id., p. 246 et seq.
26. Id., p. 250 et seq.
27. Ministerial Declaration on the Uruguay Round, GATT/1396, 25 September 1986. For an analysis of the interest constellation in the GATT discussions, see Sauvant, pp. 258 et seq.
28. According to Sauvant, p. 293.
29. By the International Telecommunications Users Group, Sauvant, p. 294.
30. For an account of the activities of UNCTC see Sauvant, p. 296 et seq.
31. Haeck, TDF Issues Vital for International Airlines, p. 7, has advocated the adoption of a new annex to the Chicago Convention in order to harmonize the free flow of data required by flag carriers.

serve the passenger as well as they facilitate the operation of the airlines.[32] On the other hand there is a reasonable interest of the passenger that his personal data be protected and not be used for purposes not related with his flight, at least not without his consent.

These objectives are certainly hard to reconcile and will require some compromise. Probably an additional instrument complementing a global framework on TDF and addressing the specific issues particular to CRSs would be the best solution.

32. Eser, Impact of Automation, p. 11.

CONCLUDING REMARKS

Airlines and their passengers have an interest in common as far as CRSs are concerned: choice among alternatives, i.e. competition in the CRS industry.

Competition is the most effective protection against dominating market power of those few who control this essential distribution tool. Governmental regulation is slow and reactive and therefore of limited use. International cooperation can be instrumental in facilitating competition on an international basis.

Passengers will benefit from competition because it will result in continuing efforts to improve CRSs and it will allow passengers to avoid bias and other factors that work to their detriment. Airlines will benefit from CRS competition because it will prevent unfair abuses of CRS market power in the air transport industry.

Even the airline CRS owners will benefit from CRS competition: without it there is always the threat of divestiture imposed on them by governments in order to put and end to potential or actual abuses.

Governments and consumer organizations will be called upon to raise the passengers' awareness of the tremendous importance of CRSs and of the need to avail themselves of the benefits of competition.

ANNEX A

IATA

GUIDE TO AUTOMATION
Areas 2 and 3 edition
Issued: November 1984

GLOSSARY OF TERMS

- AGENCY ADMINISTRATION means the division of IATA responsible for the administrative management and development of the IATA Agency Programme.
- AGENT means an IATA Approved Passenger Sales Agent.
- AIR CARRIER means an airline operating scheduled passenger services which may or may not be an IATA member.
- AIRLINE means an Air Carrier, operating schedules passenger services, which is not a member of IATA, but which participates in Bank Settlement Plans.
- APPROVED LOCATION (sometimes referred to as 'Location') includes Head Office and Branch Office Locations appearing on the Agency List.
- AREA SETTLEMENT PLAN (ASP) means the equivalent system in the USA to the IATA Bank Settlement Plan (BSP). It is administered by ATC.
- ATA means the Air Transportation Association of America.
- ATC means the Air Traffic Conference of America, which is the Traffic Disivion of ATA.
- AUTOMATED NEUTRAL TICKETING SCHEME means a scheme which enables an Agent with automated ticketing equipment to issue Neutral Tickets on behalf of Air Carriers participating in that scheme.
- AUTOMATED TICKET means any form of Passenger Ticket and Baggage Check described in IATA Resolutions 722 and 722a, and Recommended Practice 1722c, designed for issue in various ticket printing devices for which data may be computer-generated.
- AUTOMATED TICKETING SERVICES AGREEMENT means an

agreement between Air Carriers which permits the System of a Servicing Airline to issue Neutral Tickets on behalf of itself and a number of other Air Carriers.

- BANK SETTLEMENT PLAN (BSP) means the method of providing Agents in a particular country, or area, with Standard Traffic Documents and Neutral Tickets, and for accounting of issues, and for centrally settling accounts between Members, Airlines and Agents. It is administered by IATA.
- BAR CODE means a series of vertical bars incorporating a machine-readable coding system, using a combination of thick and thin lines, alternating with blank spaces to represent numeric characters.
- BULL'S EYE means the target symbol consisting of a circle with a centre dot, following the check digit on audit coupons, to provide optical character recognition (OCR) identification of the 13 digit Document Number.

- CATHODE RAY TUBE (CRT) – See Visual Display Unit (VDU).
- CLOSED USER GROUP means selected or subscribing Persons who are linked to a master System generaly via videotex, and who have access or information display capabilities.
- CO-HOST AIRLINE (CARRIER) means an Air Carrier whose schedules and availability are stored and displayed, on a preferential basis, in the System of another Air Carrier. A co-host arrangement may include additional features.
- CO-ORDINATOR means the Person appointed by the Air Carriers participating in a Neutral Ticketing Scheme for the administration of that Scheme.

- DESIGNATED PRINTER means the manufacturer of Neutral Tickets.
- DIRECT ACCESS SYSTEM means the system which enables a user to have real time direct access to other Air Carrier Systems, through a Prime Host Airline system.
- DOCUMENT NUMBER means a unique identification number of a Traffic Document, comprising the airline code, form code and serial number.

- FLOPPY DISK means a magnetic disc unit using a single plate flexible discpack. Often used for loading 'read only' storage displays.

- GATEWAY means the access from one System to another System or switching device that enables entry into the System.

- HOSTED AIRLINE (CARRIER) means an Air Carrier which utilises the facilities of another System to process, on an inventory basis, reservations and other passenger related information.

- INTERFACE means a translation function between a user and a System, or between a user and a number of Systems, or between two or more Systems.

- JOINT AUTOMATED AGENCY TICKETING AGREEMENT means an agreement between Air Carriers, enabling Agents operating auto-mated ticketing systems to issue Neutral Tickets on their behalf.

- LOZENGE means a rectangular symbol with curved-in sides following the check digit on flight coupons, to provide optical character recognition (OCR) identification of the 13-digit Document Number.

- MAGNETIC STRIPE means a stripe of magnetic material affixed to the back of a Computer Ticket, or an Automated Ticket/Boarding Pass, on which most of the data relevant to that ticket is magnetically encoded, and is machine readable.
- MEMBER means an Air Carrier which is a Member of IATA.
- MULTI ACCESS SYSTEM means a System which enables a user to have real time direct access to a variety of Air Carrier Systems through a common switching centre and/or interface.
- MULTI ACCESS TICKETING means a System whereby an Agent (with a Visual Display Unit (VDU) and a Ticket Printer) has access to the reservations and ticketing functions of two or more Air Carriers. The Agent can issue tickets of those Air Carriers on its Ticket Printer.
- MULTI HOST SYSTEM means a System that provides more than one Air Carrier with the facility to process, on an inventory basis, reservations and other passenger related functions.

- NEUTRAL TICKET means the form of Automated Ticket (governed by Resolution 722a) intended for use by Agents, not bearing any pre-printed Air Carrier identity.

- OFF-PREMISE LOCATION means any non airline location, e.g. an approved location of a Passenger Sales Agent or a commercial account.
- OFF-PREMISE TRANSITIONAL AUTOMATED TICKET (OPTAT) means the ticket described in Resolution 722a, and intended for use by Agents, whether or not this bears a preprinted individual Air Carrier identity.

- OPTICAL CHARACTER RECOGNITION (OCR) means a system for automatic reading of Document Numbers or other data, using a machine-readable type font.

- PASSENGER NAME RECORD (PNR) means a record of each passenger's travel requirements, which contains all information necessary to enable reservations to be processed and controlled by the booking Air Carrier and Air Carrier(s) participating in the carriage.
- PERSON means an individual, partnerships, firm, association, company or corporation.
- PLAN MANAGEMENT means the department of IATA responsible to the Agency Administrator for the administrative management, and development, of the BSP in the different areas where it is applicable. The term 'Plan Management' includes the local representative in the area of the BSP (BSP Manager).
- PRIME HOST AIRLINE (CARRIER) means the Air Carrier which controls the System in which other Air Carriers are hosted.

- RECEIVE ONLY (RO) pertaining to a terminal device having a printing or display mechanism but no means of transmission, e.g. Ticket Printer.

- SERVICING AIRLINE means an Air Carrier whose System is used to print (or to acquire ticketing data in order to print) Neutral Tickets, either on its own behalf, or on behalf of other Air Carriers.
- SERVICING AIRLINE CODE means a four-digit code comprising a three-numeric code plus a check digit of the servicing Air Carrier System generating the ticketing transmission. This code is always transmitted by the generating System, either directly or through a third party.
- SET – See Visual Display Unit (VDU).
- SINGLE ACCESS SYSTEM means a System in which a user has direct access to a single Air Carrier's System which may or may not provide reservations and/or ticketing capabilities on other Air Carriers.
- STAND-ALONE SYSTEM means an Agent's system which is used for recording bookings and reservations but is not linked to principals' Systems (also sometimes referred to as an Agent's 'mini system').
- STANDARD TRAFFIC DOCUMENT means any traffic document supplied to an Agent for issue under a BSP.
- STOCK CONTROL NUMBER means the unique identification number that is preprinted on Automated Tickets not having preprinted form and serial numbers.
- SYSTEM means an automated method, including equipment and

programmes, for performing reservations functions and/or for the issuance of tickets.

- SYSTEM DESCRIPTION means a written specification of the functions and mode of operation of the System.
- SYSTEM PROVIDER means the Person approved by the Air Carriers as supplier(s) of the System.

- TERMINAL – See Visual Display Unit (VDU).
- TICKETING AIRLINE means an Air Carrier whose Automated Tickets are issued through a System by imprinting the Ticketing Airline's name and numeric code.
- TICKETING AIRLINE SELECTION RULES means the rules governing the selection, by the Agent, of the Air Carrier to be designated as the Ticketing Airline on a Neutral Ticket.
- TICKET PRINTER means a computer driven machine that imprints ticketing data on a Traffic Document in the prescribed format.
- TICKETING INFORMATION EXCHANGE STANDARD (TIES) means the ATA/IATA standard which defines specifications for the exchange of ticketing information between Air Carriers.
- TRAFFIC DOCUMENTS means the following forms issued manually, mechanically or electronically for air passenger transportation over the lines of the Member or Airline and for related services, whether or not they bear a preprinted individual Member's identification: (a) Passenger Ticket and Baggage Check forms, Miscellaneous Charges Orders and On-Line Tickets supplied by Members to Approved Agents for issue to their customers, and (b) Standard Passenger Ticket forms, Standard Miscellaneous Charges Orders and other accountable forms supplied to Approved Agents for issue under the Bank Settlement Plan.
- TRANSITIONAL AUTOMATED TICKET (TAT) means the ticket described in Resolution 722.
- TRANSMISSION CONTROL NUMBER means a unique reference number generated by the ticketing System, and printed on an Automated Ticket.

- VISUAL DISPLAY UNIT (VDU) means a television-type screen on which characters are displayed, which may have been entered by use of a keyboard or automatic reading device or transmitted by a System to which the VDU is linked.

ANNEX B

14 CFR Chapter II

Part 255 – Carrier owned Computer Reservation Systems
(U.S. CAB 1984 CRS Rules)

GLOSSARY OF TERMS

Part I

(Regulation ER-1385)

14 CFR Chapter II

PART 255 – CARRIER-OWNED COMPUTER RESERVATION SYSTEMS

Section 255.1 *Purpose*

(a) The purpose of this part is to set forth requirements for operation by air carriers of computer reservation systems used by subscribers so as to prevent unfair, deceptive, predatory, and anticompetitive practices in air transportation.

(b) Nothing in this part operates to exempt any person from the operation of the antitrust laws set forth in subsection (a) of the first section of the Clayton Act (15 U.S.C. sec. 12).

Section 255.2 *Applicability*

This rule applies to air carriers and foreign air carriers that own, control or operate computerized reservations systems for subscribers in the United States, and the sale in the United States of interstate, overseas, and foreign passenger air transportation through such systems.

Section 255.3 *Definitions*

'Affiliate' means any person owned by, controlled by, or under common control with a carrier.

'Availability' means information provided in display with respect to the seats a carrier holds out as available for sale on a particular flight.

'Carrier' means any air carrier, any foreign air carrier, and any commuter air carrier, as defined in 49 U.S.C. 1301(3), 49 U.S.C. 1301 (22), and 14 CFR sec. 298.2(f), respectively that are engaged directly in the operation of aircraft in passenger air transportation.

'Discriminate', 'Discrimination' and 'discriminatory' mean, respectively, to discriminate unjustly, unjust discrimination, and unjustly discriminatory.

'Display' means the system's presentation of carrier schedules, fares, rules or availability to a subscriber by means of a computer terminal.

'Participating carrier' means a carrier that has an agreement with a system vendor for display of its flight schedules, fares, or seat availability, or for the making of reservations or issuance of tickets through a system.

'Primary display' means any display presented by a system vendor to comply with section 255.4.

'Service enhancement' means any product or service offered to subscribers or passengers in conjunction with a system other than the display of information schedules, fares, rules, and availability, and the ability to make reservations or to issue tickets for air transportation.

'Subscriber' means a ticket agent, as defined in 49 U.S.C. 1301(40) of the Act, that holds itself out as a neutral source of information about, or tickets for, the air transportation industry and that uses a system.

'System' means a computerized airline reservation system offered by a carrier or its affiliate to subscribers for use in the United States that contains information about schedules, fares, rules or availability of other carriers and that provides subscribers with the ability to make reservations and to issue tickets.

'System vendor' means a carrier or its affiliate that owns, controls or operates a system.

Section 255.4 *Display of information*

(a) All systems shall provide a primary display or primary displays that include the schedules, fares, rules and availability of all carriers in accordance with the provisions of this section. Primary displays shall be at least as useful for subscribers, in terms of functions or enhancements offered, and the ease with which such functions or enhancements can be performed or implemented, as any other displays maintained by the system vendor.

(b) In ordering the information contained in a primary display, system vendors shall not use any factors directly or indirectly relating to carrier identity.

(1) System vendors may order the display of information on the basis of

any service criteria that do not reflect carrier identity and that are consistently applied to all carriers, including the system vendor, and to all markets.

(2) System vendors shall provide upon request to all subscribers and participating carriers the current criteria used in ordering flights for the primary displays and the weight given to each criterion.

(c) System vendors shall not use any factors directly or indirectly relating to carrier identity in constructing the primary displays of connecting flights.

(1) System vendors may select the connecting points to be used in the construction of connecting flights for each city pair on the basis of any service criteria that do not reflect carrier identity and that are applied consistently to all carriers, including the system vendor, and to all markets.

(2) System vendors may select connecting flights for inclusion ('edit') on the basis of service criteria that do not reflect carrier identity and that are applied consistently to all carriers, including the system vendor.

(3) System vendors shall provide upon request to all subscribers and participating carriers current information on:

(i) all connecting points used for each market;
(ii) all criteria used to select connecting points;
(iii) all criteria used to 'edit' connecting flights; and
(iv) the weight given to each criterion in (ii) and (iii) above.

(d) Upon receipt of information from any carrier, system vendors shall apply the same standards of care and timeliness to loading information concerning participating carriers as it applies to the loading of its own information.

(1) If a system vendor provides special loading capability to any other carrier, it shall offer the same capability to all participating carriers in a non-discriminatory fashion as soon as technically feasible.

(2) Each system vendor shall provide upon request to all participating carriers all current data base update procedures and data formats.

Section 255.5 *Contracts with participating carriers*

(a) No system vendor shall discriminate among participating carriers in the fees for participation in its system, or for system related services. Differing fees to participating carriers for the same of similar levels of service shall be presumed to be discriminatory.

(b) No system vendor shall condition participation in its system on the purchase or sale of any other goods or services.

(c) System vendors shall provide upon request to carriers current information on their fee levels and fee arrangements with other participating carriers.

Section 255.6 *Contracts with subscribers*

(a) No subscriber contract shall have a term in excess of five years.

(b) No system vendor shall directly or indirectly prohibit a subscriber from obtaining or using any other system.

(c) No system vendor shall require use of its system, by the subscriber in any sale of its air transportation services.

(d) No system vendor shall require that a travel agent use its system as a condition for the receipt of any commission for the sale of its air transportation services.

(e) No system vendor shall charge prices to subscribers conditioned in whole or in part on the identity of carriers whose flights are sold by the subscriber.

Section 255.7 *Service enhancements*

In the event that a system vendor offers a service enhancement to any participating carrier, it shall offer it to all participating carriers on non-discriminatory terms.

Section 255.8 *Marketing information*

Each system vendor shall make available to all participating carriers on non-discriminatory terms all marketing, booking and sales data that it elects to generate from its system.

Section 255.9 *Exceptions*

(a) The obligations of a system vendor under section 255.4 shall not apply with respect to a carrier that refuses to enter into a contract that complies with this part or fails to pay a non-discriminatory fee. A system vendor shall apply its policy concerning treatment of non-paying carriers on a uniform basis to all such carriers, and shall not receive payment from any carrier for system-related services unless such payments are made pursuant to a contract complying with this part.

(b) The obligations of a system vendor under this part shall not apply to any foreign air carrier that operates or whose affiliate operates an airline computer reservation system for travel agents outside the United States that does not display the flights of all United States carriers equally with the flights of the foreign carrier.

Section 255.10 *Review and termination*

(a) The Federal agency administering this rule shall conduct as review within 5 years after its effective date.

(b) Unless extended on the basis of the review specified above, this rule shall terminate on December 31, 1990.

Part II

(Regulation ER-1395)

Amendment No. 2
to 14 CFR Part 255

. . .
2. A new section 255.4(c) (4) is added, to read:
Section 255.4 Display of information

. . .
  (c) . . .
(4) If system vendors select connecting points for use in constructing connecting flights they shall use at least nine points for each city-pair, except that vendors may select fewer than nine such connecting points for city-pair where --
(i) Fewer than nine connecting points meet the service criteria described in paragraph (c)(1) of this section; and
(ii) The vendor has used all the points that meet those criteria, along with all additional connecting points requested by participating carriers.

Part III

(Regulation ER-1396)

Amendment No. 3
to 14 CFR Part 255

. . .
2. Section 255.4, *Display of information*, is amended by deleting the phrase 'to all subscribers and participating carriers' where it appears, and substituting the phrase 'to any person', so that it would read as follows:

Section 255.4 *Display of information*
. . .
  (1) . . .
(2) System vendors shall provide to any person upon request the current criteria used in ordering flights for the primary displays and the weights given to each criterion.
  (c) . . .

(3) System vendors shall provide to any person upon request current information on:

(i) all connecting points used for each market;

(ii) all criteria used to select connecting points;

(iii) all criteria used to 'edit' connecting flights; and

(iv) the weight given to each criterion in paragraphs (c)(3)(ii) and (iii) of this section.

(d) . . .

(2) Each system vendor shall provide to any person upon request all current data base update procedures and data formats.

3. Paragraph (a) of section 255.8, *Marketing information*, is amended, and a new paragraph (b) is added so that it will read as follows:

Section 255.8 *Marketing information*

(a) With the exception of marketing, booking, and sales data relating to the international operations of any carrier, each system vendor shall make available to all U.S. participating carriers on non-discriminatory terms all marketing, booking, and sales data relating to U.S. carriers that it elects to generate from its system.

(b) System vendors and participating carriers shall not release marketing, booking, and sales data they generate or receive relating to international operations of any carrier, absent authorization to do so by the carrier.

ANNEX C

ICAO Document FRP/9

Panel of Experts on the Machinery for the Establishment of
International Fares and Rates

Ninth Meeting
Montréal, 24 November – 5 December, 1986

Report

Appendices 3 and 4

APPENDIX 3

Examples of CRS Display Bias

Bias Factor	Example
Individual carrier identity	Displaying flights/fares for carrier 'YY' ahead of those for carrier 'XX' by means of over-ride of other display priority parameters. Displaying fares for carrier 'YY' in addition to those for carrier 'XX' whenever fares for carrier 'XX' are requested.
Nationality of carrier	Displaying flights/fares for carrier 'YY' ahead of those for carrier 'XX' because 'YY' is a national carrier.
Carrier's status of participation in CRS	Because carrier 'XX' is not a co-host, not enabling any enhancements for carrier 'XX' through the system. Similarly, because 'XX' is not a participating carrier: a) excluding from the display flights by

carrier 'XX' which compete with those of carrier 'YY', connecting flights by carrier 'XX' ('XX'/'XX', 'XX'/'ZZ' or, less frequently, 'XX'/'YY'), or all flights by carrier 'XX';

b) displaying flights by carrier 'XX' after those of participating carrier 'YY';

c) not enabling reservations or ticketing for carrier 'XX' through the system.

Airport identity	Displaying flights/fares from airport 'XXX' ahead of those from airport 'YYY' by means of over-ride of other screen priority parameters.
Commonality of screen priority parameters	Applying the same screen priority parameters to domestic, domestic/international and purely international services, despite the distinctive characteristics of these services.
Definition (or price for listing) of connecting flights	Limiting the number of alternative connections which may be listed, or excluding from the display some or all connecting flights through a particular city because they do not meet specified connection parameters (such as the volume of traffic through that city) and/or because the price for listing the connecting flights concerned is unreasonably high.
Priority given to on-line transfers	Displaying carrier 'YY'/carrier 'YY' connection ahead of carrier 'XX'/carrier 'ZZ' or carrier 'YY'/carrier 'ZZ' connection despite other inferior connection parameters for the former (*note:* where the connection is domestic/international, a wholly domestic carrier or a foreign international carrier thereby loses display priority).
Code-sharing	Carrier 'XX' and carrier 'ZZ' making agreement for designation of carrier 'XX'/

	carrier 'ZZ' connection as carrier 'XX' / carrier 'XX' in order to retain priority under above parameters.
Dual-listing	In previous circumstances separate, additional listing (using different flight parameters if necessary to avoid detection) of carrier 'XX' flight for local traffic purposes.
Restrictions on display of fares	Limiting the number of classes of service or types of fare which may be listed (in some instances fewer classes have been available for participating carriers than for a vendor carrier).
Change of gauge without change of flight number	Retention of single flight number where a change of aircraft is required en-route in order to achieve display priority. This practice can also lead to dual or multiple listing where there are several feeder services for a long-haul service with the same flight number.
Departure time Arrival time Length of flight time	Falsification of flight schedules by carriers, individually or jointly, in order to achieve display priority.

APPENDIX 4

Examples of Market Manipulation by CRS Vendors
Other than through Display Bias

Item	*Example*
Control of participation	Outright refusal to accept a (foreign) carrier as a participant, or acceptance only under burdensome or discriminatory conditions.
Control of sales information	a) Manipulation of a participating carrier's fare and flight information to that carrier's disadvantage. b) Evaluation of and response to a compet-

	ing carrier's revised schedules and fares before they are officially announced.
Control of marketing information	Information generated through a CRS exclusively available to vendor or sold only at excessive fees (including, for example, data to identify travel agents who might be induced to direct their business away from competing carriers or analyses of reservation patterns with a view to amending tariffs).
Control of reservations policy	Reservations for flights on routes where vendor is a dominant or monopoly carrier conditioned upon use of the same carrier wherever available for any other segments of the journey.
Control of ticket validation	Designation of vendor as validating carrier on all tickets or on any ticket containing a coupon for that carrier (whether first coupon or not) in order to achieve improved cash flow.
Control of system enhancements	'Last seat' availability or advance issue of boarding passes available only for vendor carrier.
Tying of agents to a single access system	a) Prohibition of agent's use of other systems. b) Limits on the number of reservation terminals for other CRSs permitted on agent's premises. c) Mandatory use of a vendor carrier's CRS for all reservations that contain a flight segment for that carrier (whether first segment or not).
Tying of CRS services to other arrangements	a) Provision of CRS services tied to net ticketing arrangements. b) Provision of CRS services tied to use of vendor's ticket printer (or excessive charges imposed for connection and testing of other ticket printers).

Inequitable access fees	a) Inequitable allocation of costs amongst vendor, participating carriers and travel agents.
	b) Fee structures that vary amongst participating carriers.
	c) Excessive fees for enhancement facilities.
Unreasonable contract termination clauses	a) Excessively long term of contract.
	b) Excessive 'liquidated damages' for withdrawal and/or change to another CRS by agents.

BIBLIOGRAPHY

The left-hand column shows the works as they appear in the footnotes.

Atwater Institute,
   Aims, Projects and People

Atwater Institute – The World Information Economy Centre, Aims, Projects and People. Montréal, undated.

Author unknown,
   Airline Data Exchange
   Endangered?

Author unknown, Airline Data Exchange Endangered?, *Transnational Data and Communications Report*, February 1986, p. 5.

Author unknown,
   United to Implement
   $1-Billion System

Author unknown, United to Implement $1-Billion Automated Reservation System. *Aviation Week & Space Technology*, November 3, 1986, pp. 81-82.

Bittlinger,
   Conference 1985

Horst Bittlinger, Lloyd's of London Press, International Civil Aviation Conference No. 7, Den Haag, 24. und 25. Oktober 1985. *Zeitschrift für Luft- und Weltraumrecht*, 1986, pp. 45-49.

Boberg/Collison,
   CRSs and Competition

Kevin B. Boberg and Frederick M. Collison, Computer Reservation Systems and Airline Competition. Tourism Management, September 1985, pp. 174-183.

CAB,
   Report to Congress

Civil Aeronautics Board, Report on the Implications of CRS. In: U.S. Congress, House, Committee on Public Works and Transportation, Review of Airline Deregulation and Sunset of the Civil Aeronautics Board (Airline Computer Reservations Systems), Hearings before the Subcommittee on Aviation and the House Committee on Public Works and Transportation 98 Congress, 1st Session, 1983.

Department of Justice,
   1985 Report

U.S. Department of Justice, 1985 Report to Congress on the Airline Computer Reservation System Industry. December 1985, Washington, D.C.

Durbin,
Application for Satellites

Fran Durbin, Lines Prepare Application Kit for Satellites. *Travel Weekly,* December 12, 1985, pp. 1, 2.

Eser,
Impact of Automation

Günther O. Esser, Impact of Automation on the Airline Business. *Annals of Air and Space Law,* vol. XI, 1986, Paris, Pedone, pp. 3-15.

Fahy,
Regulation

Richard J. Fahy, Jr., Regulation of Computerized Reservation Systems in the United States and Europe. *Air Law,* 1986, pp. 232-241.

Feazel,
European Airlines Express
Concern

Michael Feazel, European Airlines Express Concern over Competition from Sabre, Apollo. *Aviation Week & Space Technology,* November 3, 1986, pp. 101-104.

Feldman,
CRS Controversy Grows

Joan M. Feldman, CRS Controversy Grows as Systems Become More Powerful. *Air Transport World,* 8/1986, p. 33-39.

Feldman,
The Fight is on

Joan M. Feldman, The Fight is on for a Neutral CRS. *Air Transport World,* January 1, 1985, pp. 62-64.

Godwin,
Air Canada Sets Rebates

Nadine Godwin, Air Canada Sets Agency Rebates for Air Sales on Its Reservec. *Travel Weekly,* February 2, 1987, pp. 1, 4.

Godwin,
Documents Show Lines'
Priorities

Nadine Godwin, Documents Show Lines' Priorities in Reservations Systems Displays. *Travel Weekly,* March 25, 1985, pp. 1, 4.

Godwin,
Judge Includes Liquidated
Damages

Nadine Godwin, Judge Includes Liquidated Damages in Award to AAC. *Travel Weekly,* March 16, 1987, pp. 1, 71.

Grey,
The Elements

Rodney de C. Grey, The Elements of a General Agreement on Information Transfer/Trade (GAIT). Atwater Institute, Montréal, 1986.

Haeck,
Les Flux de Données

Louis Haeck, Les Flux de Données Transfrontières et les Lignes Aériennes de

	l'IATA. In: Proceedings of the Second World Conference on Transborder Data Flow Policies sponsored by the Intergovernmental Bureau for Informatics, 1985, Rome, pp. 47 et seg.
Hammarskjöld, Conceptual Evaluation	Knut Hammarskjöld, Conceptual Evolution Caused – and Necessitated – by Technological Advancement: Transition to Information-Based Society: A Case in Point. *Annals of Air and Space Law*, 1986, vol. XI, Pedone, Paris, pp. 205-217.
Henderson, CRS Vendors Target Travel Agents	Danna K. Henderson, CRS Vendors Target Travel Agents with New Business Automation Systems. *Air Transport World*, 1986, no. 8, pp. 40 et seq.
Hurley, Mighty Apollo	Gerald Hurley, Mighty Apollo, United (*United Airlines' inflight magazine*), September 1986.
IATA, Guide to Automation	IATA, Guide to Automated Reservations and Ticketing Systems, 'Guide to Automation', Areas 2 and 3 Edition. November 1984.
Lassiter, Scocozza Details Plans	Eric Lassiter, Scocozza Details Plans of Res Case. *Travel Weekly*, December 15, 1986, pp. 1, 4.
Levere, European Lines	Jane Levere, SAS, 3 Other Lines Eye Combined Res System. *Travel Weekly*, April 16, 1987, pp. 1, 69.
Ott, Commercial Aviation	James Ott, Commercial Aviation Enters Era of Expanded Automation. *Aviation Week & Space Technology*, November 3, 1986, p. 68.
Poling, DOT Blames Airlines	Bill Poling, DOT's Scocozza Blames Airlines' Traffic Backups on Res Displays. *Travel Weekly*, March 5, 1987, pp. 1, 41.
Poling, Federal Units Weigh Bias Rules	Bill Poling, Federal Units Weigh Bias Rules, but Changes Deemed Premature. *Travel Weekly*, March 25, 1985, pp. 1, 97.

Raben,
    CRS

Renton,
    Technology Threatens
    Travel Agents

Renton/Gaudin,
    Reserving Judgment

Roy,
    Reservec II

Sauvant,
    International Transactions

Shifrin,
    American's Parent
    Company

Sturken,
    American Considering
    Home Computer Link

Sturken,
    Covia Corp.

Sturken,
    Delta Unveils

U.S. Department of Justice,
    1985 Report

H. Raben, Computer Reservation System.
Europair, 1986, pp. 23-25.

Jane Renton, Technology Threatens Travel
Agents. *Airline Business*, April 1986, pp.
16-21.

Jane Renton/Pat Gaudin, Reserving Judgment. *Airline Business*, March 1987, pp.
18-23.

Maurice Roy, Reservec II: Putting the
World at Your Fingertips. *En Route Maga-
zine* (Air Canada), April 1987, pp. 44 et
seq.

Karl P. Sauvant, International Transactions
in Services. The Politics of Transborder
Data Flows (The Atwater Series on the
World Information Economy). 1986, Boul-
der, Westview Press.

Carole A. Shifrin, American's Parent Company Developing Automation Products,
Computer Services. *Aviation Week &
Space Technology*, November 3, 1986, p.
71-79.

Barbara Sturken, American Considering
Home Computer Link with Ticket Machines. *Travel Weekly*, December 12,
1985, pp. 1, 4.

Barbara Sturken, Covia Corp. Tests New
Res System. *Travel Weekly*, April 13, 1987,
pp. 1/2.

Barbara Sturken, Delta Unveils Multi-
faceted Res System. *Travel Weekly*, February 23, 1987, pp. 1, 4.

See Department of Justice, 1985 Report.